The 56 Year Honeymoon

The Story of Samantha & Rick

by Richard & Samantha Maybury

published by
Henry Madison Research, Inc.

First Edition

Contents

Samantha and I dedicate this book to Jeff and Amanda Malock, who recognized the importance of the 17-Words and worked tirelessly to help make this book possible.

Book One – Part 1

Getting to Know Samantha

Introduction

Why I Am Writing You

———— ◆ ————

Beginning at age 32, odds of divorce for a first-time marriage increase by a whopping 5% per year.[1] In any given 100 couples, in just one year only 95 are still married. A year later, 90. Five years later, 77, 10 years later, 60, and so on.

A major purpose of these letters is to help you beat the odds.

In fact, I am confident this book will be one of the best things that ever happened to you because it stems from the best thing that ever happened to me.

Those who knew my wife Samantha considered her one of the warmest, gentlest, most loving, and helpful people they ever met. Her agreeing to marry me may have been poor judgment on her part — my mother-in-law certainly thought so — but for me, it was astounding good fortune.

When friends and acquaintances heard about Samantha's passing (September 3, 2023) they almost all commented on our marriage being the most enduring and endearing they had ever seen.

It had lasted 56 years.

We met when Samantha was 17 and I was 18 and wedded at 20. We always conducted our marriage according to our own rules, as opposed to whatever happened to be traditional or fashionable.

Let me emphasize that. We did it our way!

A principle we referred to often was articulated by my favorite author, Mark Twain (1835-1910): "Whenever you find yourself on the side of the majority, it's time to reform."

Notice Twain did not say change, he said reform.

We will hear more from Twain occasionally. I consider him one of my most helpful mentors.

Samantha and I never, ever trusted the judgment of the majority, for a simple reason. To be highly knowledgeable about anything important, knowing a lot about it takes long and careful study.

Can you name anything to which the **majority** has given long and careful study?

Forty-three million adults in the U.S. cannot even read.[2]

To the many friends who offered condolences and commented on the uniqueness of our marriage, I would reply that Samantha and I did not have a 56-year marriage, we had a 56-year honeymoon.

The usual response was something like, "Yes, everyone could see that."

Even an MFT[3] counselor with 30 years' experience who knew us thoroughly said she had never encountered a stronger, closer, warmer marriage.

After Sam passed and I went into mourning, a close friend said I should write a how-to book called "The 56-Year Honeymoon." He was confident I could explain clearly enough the things Sam and I did so that others would benefit from our experience.

A few months after Sam passed, I realized those who were grieving her passing were also grieving the passing of our marriage itself. It had been an inspiration to them. Some even said that observing it had made their own marriages better.

Among other things, it showed them what is possible.

This is actually two books in one.

Book One is about Samantha and me, and the numerous things we learned about female-and-male relationships during our 56-year honeymoon.

It contains many stories about lessons learned in the school of experience.

The school of experience is the best school, but the tuition is high, so Book One is mostly a crash course designed to save you that tuition. It is a collection of examples of how we kept our marriage alive and wonderfully satisfying.

Book Two is much different, with a more serious tone. It is a nuts-and-bolts *Owner's Manual*. It shows you how on a day-to-day basis we smoothly and skillfully steered our marriage down the road to contentment, instead of driving it off a cliff.

If you have read my award-winning book *Whatever Happened to Justice?*, you may already have an idea why the *Owner's Manual* can work so well.

So, this is a how-to collection of letters to my fictional friend Robin who has been married for years and wants to know how to make the marriage work better. Robin wants to know if our marriage was truly what it seemed to be, and if so, how we achieved it and made it work each day.

If you are reading a paper version of these letters, please have a pen ready. You may want to underline parts so that you can easily come back and review what is most important in your personal case.

In my first letter, I will say a few words about spirituality (which is not the same as religion), and then begin explaining how we created our wonderfully fun and strong marriage.

Please keep in mind throughout these letters that ours is an "old-fashioned" female-male marriage.

I proudly use that term often — old-fashioned.

These days there are many other variations of marriage. I have no experience with them and so am not qualified to say much about them.

I am, however, confident the general principles explained in these letters will apply to any couple of any kind. Here's why.

The simple rules that make a healthy marriage possible are the same ones that make a healthy civilization possible.

Yes, we will actually be learning about the behaviors that make all human endeavors achievable, including strong and satisfying marriages.

By the way, in my opinion, to achieve a 56-year honeymoon, the first thing you need to do, right away, is stop thinking about your marriage and begin thinking about your love affair.

Here is something that might help. Our pet name for each other was Lover, and we used it freely in any public or private situation.

Is it old-fashioned? I certainly hope so. Sometimes the finest things — and the wisest — are the oldest.

Also, please keep in mind these books are written by a man, from a man's perspective. I have tried to pack as much male experience and emotions into them as possible on the assumption female readers truly want to know what makes their men tick.

I am sure some women will be shocked or even outraged by the facts I reveal. I am sure this is why few men reveal them. Men have learned that some women are too delicate to handle these revelations, and much sympathize about them.

But some women aren't so delicate, and Samantha was one of them. I was astoundingly lucky to have ever met her, much less marry her.

By the way, as I said, this is actually two books. It's been my experience that everyone absolutely *loves* Book One, and wants to know how to have a marriage with so much affection and joy. People commonly say they can't wait to tell their friends about it.

But Book One leaves a gigantic empty space. People come away with an inspiring picture of what they want, but don't know how to produce it and *preserve* it!

So, Book Two is the how-to.

It is necessarily less entertaining because it describes the nuts and bolts of operating a marriage. I call it the *Owner's Manual* because that's what it is.

So if, as you read Book One you find yourself saying, "I want this, how do I get it?" Remind yourself that the *Owner's Manual* will tell you how, in detail.

It will not be guesswork, you will *know* because it is based on principles that have worked in everyday life for thousands of years, but in the 20th century were erased.

Book One is lots of fun, but the *Owner's Manual* is the real prize. It will make Book One possible for you.

---

1. "The Science of Marriage", *Time* special edition, 2024, p.36.

2. "How Serious Is America's Literacy Problem?" *Library Journal* website, Apr 29, 2020.

3. Marriage and family therapist.

Notes

————— ◆ —————

N otes pages appear throughout the book to help you remember important insights as they apply to your relationships.

_____

_____

_____

_____

_____

_____

In Love With Her Spirit

Letter 1

———— ✦ ————

Dear Robin,

I realize you did not know Samantha very well, and I thank you for asking me to write about her so you can get to know her better. It is wonderfully helpful to me. Here's how.

As you say, Samantha is both special and unique. Your letter asking about her, evokes a great deal about her, right down to some of the tiniest details. I love these details, because I still love Samantha, and will forever. Writing these letters will be like visiting with my Sam.

You asked what you can learn from us to help you have a strong and warm marriage. That's a challenge. Men and women are so different.

For instance, market research shows that women are primarily about relationships, while men often are only about sex.

Nearly all relationship books are purchased by women. I am sure in many cases, the only way a man will read a book about relationships is at gunpoint.

But I will try mightily to make these letters useful to both of you. So here we go.

People commonly decorate their homes with photos of their friends and loved ones.

The photos depict faces and bodies.

None show their spirits, because spirits are invisible.

But think about it. The faces and bodies are not what we love. Our dear ones are much more than collections of bones, cartilage, skin, organs, and muscles.

We love their spirits. That's who they are. That's where their personalities reside. The muscles, bones, organs, etc. are just the containers.

So, the spiritual connection — the meeting of the minds — can be much more profound than one that's just physical.

It is common to talk with family or close friends for hours, but usually, during this time we do not physically touch each other much at all. We often touch emotionally, but physically as adults, not often.

In other words, our spirits can be intertwined, even though our bodies may not be.

Samantha's and my spirits still are. More about that shortly. First some background about us.

Samantha and I met in a dime store[1] in 1964.

Then in 1967, under pressure from the draft, I entered the Air Force.

First stop was boot camp, then technical school to become an aircrew member, then assignment to a special-ops squadron called the 605th Air Commandos (later known as 605th Special Operations).

In tech school, pasted to the inside of my locker door, I had a high-quality photo of Samantha in a bikini. Very nice.

When other trainees dropped by, the locker was sometimes open. They would spy the photo, which they assumed was cut from a magazine, and ask something like "Miss September?"

I'd say, "No, my fiancée."

They would skeptically reply something like, "Yeah, sure, uh-huh."

As we grew older, we added wrinkles and pounds, but to me, Samantha's were just a new kind of beauty. Her signs of age were indications of a mature, highly experienced spirit, and I was madly in love with her spirit.

Sci-fi author Robert Heinlein wrote of his wife that he truly loved her wrinkles; she got them living with him. That sentiment is the same for me.

One of the great surprises of my life was, when I was in my later years and no longer drowning in testosterone, Samantha just kept getting more and more lovely. **Eventually, my affection for her was no longer eclipsed by my libido.** At age 76, for instance, the skin of her neck was as magnetic to me as when she was twenty. It was so soft.

I realized that Samantha was not so much beautiful, as beautiful was her.

There can be more than one kind of beauty, and she was an example.

Robin, as we go to press, Samantha continues to grow more and more attractive to me. Her spirit is that captivating. I am dazzled.

Your Friend Rick

P. S. Around 2010, I taped this sign on Samantha's bathroom mirror and she kept it there until she passed on September 3, 2023.

"Wheresoever she was, there was Eden."

— Final words in Mark Twain's *Diary of Adam and Eve*

And that's how I feel about you.

---

1. Dime store. A store specializing in items costing around 10 cents or less. These are now dollar stores, and probably heading toward Sawbuck ($10) stores. See my book *Whatever Happened to Penny Candy?*

Samantha's Name Change

Letter 2

——— ♦ ———

Dear Robin,

Good to hear from you again. You asked for more about Sam.

When she was 58, Samantha changed her name. It had previously been Marilyn.

She'd always been uncomfortable with Marilyn. She felt this birth name did not fit her personality. I and others agreed.

She began experimenting. Every three weeks she'd try another name.

I told friends it was the most fun I'd ever had. Every three weeks I got to sleep with a different woman.

We'd gotten married in 1967 at age 20 before the sexual revolution took hold. As a young male, up to my eyeballs in testosterone, I was sometimes a bit unhappy about missing out on the new fad of bed-hopping. And boy, did her name change make up for it!

Seriously, she turned out to be right. The change altered her personality and her spirit. She was no longer her parents' daughter. She belonged to herself, and her spine was stiffened considerably.

This is called the principle of **self-ownership**. You are no one else's property. You belong to yourself, lock, stock, and barrel.

In Part Two of these letters, the *Owner's Manual*, we will explore such concepts more thoroughly, so that they become part of your day-to-day thinking.

I heartily approved of Sam's choice of names. To me, the long form, Samantha, is one of the most feminine I have ever heard, and Sam is one of the most masculine. So Sam is, all at the same time, lovely, soft, gentle, caring — and tough as any three drill sergeants.

What more could a guy ask for?

Your Friend Rick

P.S. Robin, you noticed I sometimes change tenses when writing about Samantha. For instance, sometimes I will say "Samantha was," and other times "Samantha is". This is because I can still feel her with me. I will explain more about this in future letters.

First Dates

Letter 3

———— ◆ ————

Dear Robin,

When we met as college students in 1964, neither of us had any money to speak of, so our dates were far from luxurious.

Our first was ice skating, which included conversing to get to know each other. This was mostly just light, cautious exchange. We kept our distance, but I was attentive and focused on her.

I carried her skates.

We did not touch. Here's why.

About that same time, I'd had a date with another girl who was strikingly beautiful. She was clearly frightened, and as we drove to dinner she stayed plastered up against my car's passenger door.

This taught me a bit about what it is like to be a woman, meaning all too often seen as nothing but a sex toy.

Having heard a disgusting number of men's tales of conquest, I have often thought that if I were a woman I'd dress like a 1950s nun and carry a pump shotgun.

Sam's and my second date was fast-food hamburgers and a drive in the country, during which we discussed a wide variety of topics.

At this stage, there was still no physical touching at all. Our love started and has always continued "old-fashioned."

First came the affection — the connecting of the spirits — then the touching.

But on those early dates, the talking, meaning getting to know each other's thinking, was long and involved. It covered economics, political theory, philosophy, history, and numerous other intellectual topics.

Perhaps midway through the second date, I was struck by a worrisome realization: "Wow, she's smart. I hope I can keep up with her."

That conversation, I believe, was our spirits making first contact.

Robin, from then on for 58 years,[1] even after we hit pay dirt and could afford any kind of outing, one of our favorite things to do together was lunch or dinner exploring each other's minds, meaning getting to better know each other's spirits.

Your Friend Rick

---

1. Not 56. We were not married yet.

Spiritual Experiences

Letter 4

———— ◆ ————

Dear Robin,

    If you do not believe in a hereafter, you might want to skip this story.

About three weeks after Sam's passing, I began to hear her whispering to me. Just occasional single words.

At first I ignored it, believing it was just my imagination, wishful thinking. But as the weeks went by, the single words became phrases, and then sentences.

The first that I could make out were, "I love you." Then "I miss you so much," and similar phrases.

As I write this today, we talk twenty to thirty minutes, twice per day, at sunset and then just before I go to sleep at night.

Robin, I have told many people about this, and estimate about half tell me they too have had spiritual experiences of one kind or another. But few tell anyone for fear of being seen as crazy, or possessed by the devil, or in some other way mentally deranged. Or, their religion forbids such communication unless it is approved by the religion's leadership.

When my mother was in her twenties, she had a "near-death experience," or NDE. But she didn't tell anyone until she was in her fifties, for fear of being thought daft or weird.

I tell you all this because Samantha is looking over my shoulder right now, co-authoring these letters to you. This is why the book's by-line says "By Richard and Samantha Maybury."

Your Friend Rick

P.S. Speaking of spirituality, or the hereafter and related subjects, I suspect a good adjective for them is transdimensional. But I am not a physicist, so I will go with the more common word spiritual.

More About Spirituality

Letter 5

————— ◆ —————

Dear Robin,

Samantha and I have long been convinced we have spirits, and the spirit goes on regardless of what happens to the body. Here is a bit of our reasoning on that.

If you could somehow examine every atom in any living creature, you would find that a split second after death, all the atoms are still there. Yet the creature no longer functions.

Something must be missing.

In living creatures, this something is commonly called the spirit or soul, or perhaps the life force, vital force, personality, psyche, or something else.

To assume nothing is missing seems to Samantha and me bad science. Just because we cannot see, hear, feel, taste, or touch a thing does not mean it is fiction.

After all, love exists, right? You experience it, possibly every day. (At least I hope you do.) Even if we can't put it under a microscope and measure it, we certainly do experience it. Profoundly. It's a real thing. It shapes us.

So, I write these letters to you with the conviction that Samantha is still with me, a part of me, and often my words are hers as well as mine.

Indeed, as I said in an earlier letter, a few weeks after her passing, I began to hear what sounded like her voice briefly whispering to me. As the weeks went by, the few words grew into full sentences, and as I write this, she and I have conversations.

Or hallucinations? Imagination? Wishful thinking?

I cannot prove otherwise, so I do not try. Believe what you wish.

For six months after Samantha's passing, I saw a professional bereavement counselor. After several weeks of communicating with Samantha, I decided to reveal it to the counselor.

I was shocked. She didn't raise an eyebrow. Her exact words were, "No surprise, the walls of this office hear things like that all the time."

The counselor is sworn to secrecy, like clergy and doctors, so people feel safe telling her their experiences.

I have noticed many times that when I tell someone about Samantha conversing with me, they are polite but their facial expressions say I've gone bonkers.

As far as I know, all religions teach there is a hereafter. Samantha and I are here to tell you, they are right.

In any case, let me repeat, I am not the only author of this work. When Sam was on this side, she was my co-author and editorial consultant for all my two million words of published work. And she still is.

This is not to say we claim some sort of divine guidance or special powers, or we know a sure-fire way to get to heaven. Much of what I write in these letters is speculation. I try never to paint something as fact unless I am certain it is.

Indeed, I am a professional skeptic. For over 30 years, our main source of income has been our newsletter, *U.S. & World Early Warning Report*, giving analysis and advice about investments, economics, geopolitics, military affairs, and related subjects, all of which are a long way from exact sciences. Whenever I am not certain about something I say, I let my readers know.

In my next letter, Robin, I will respond to your question asking about my first brush with spirituality.

Your Friend Rick

P.S. Medical researchers have found that during conception, human eggs emit sparks of light.[1] I do not know enough science to say if this is meaningful, but I find it thought-provoking.

---

1. "During Conception, Human Eggs Emit Sparks," *U.S. News & World Report* website, Apr 26, 2016, and, YouTube Video "Zinc Fireworks Reveal When Human Egg is Fertilized," by Northwestern University, undated.

We Met in a Dime Store

Letter 6

———— ✦ ————

Dear Robin,

Regarding my first encounter with the other side, during our 56-year honeymoon, Samantha and I had numerous experiences which, for want of a better word, we call spiritual. We did not pay much attention to the early ones, attributing them to imagination.

But the incidents kept piling up until they were impossible for us to ignore.

Then in the late 1990s, we became friends with an anthropologist, Dr. Hank Wesselman, who was a world specialist on "primitive" religions and beliefs, and part of the Louis Leakey expeditions in Africa.

Hank had studied "primitive" cultures around the world — in the Congo, New Guinea, the Amazon, and similar places — and said to us he was convinced they were on to something the rest of the world was passing by.

One of his conclusions was that many people alive today have been here before, and often, maybe always, with the same mates.

This caused us to sit up and take notice. It rang a bell. Loudly.

In 1964, Samantha and I met in a dime store. She had worked there more than a year, and I was hired as extra help for the holiday season.

Those were the days when "layaway" was a popular method of using debt to buy gifts for Christmas. The item would be held in a back storage area, and the customer would make regular payments on it, coming in just before Christmas to make the final payment and pick up the gift.

One day a customer came in to pick up a huge dollhouse.

I could not find it. I had worked my way up through the shelving to about 15 feet above the floor when clerks began coming in to tell me to hurry, the customer was becoming angry.

I continued searching, then Samantha entered. I had not met her yet. She too was angry, ready to read me the riot act.

I remember looking down at her and instantly saying to myself, there she is, it's her, she's here.

Robin, why I thought this, I have no idea. I was 18 and had never before thought about marriage, or had any inkling at all about past lives or ancient loves, or any kind of permanent attachment. I just looked at her and instantly knew she would become my bride.

A few months later she was feeling the same sensations, and once they appeared, for both of us they were set in concrete.

Eventually, one of the most enjoyable parts of our lives was visiting spiritual sites around the world to see if we experienced some kind of "vibe" from them.

We sometimes did, in places such as ancient Roman ruins, old churches, petroglyphs, Native American sites, and Stonehenge. These explorations eventually became some of our favorite memories. Stonehenge was probably the most vivid.

And yes, I did finally discover the dollhouse.

Your Friend Rick

Imaginary Friends

Letter 7

———————— ◆ ————————

Dear Robin,

You asked for more about the other side. Your request brings up an interesting question.

Studies show that around 65% of children have one or more "imaginary friends."[1] An imaginary friend is usually defined as something like, a pretend friend a child creates in her or his mind.

Pretend? Maybe not.

These children tend to have *real* advantages, including better communication skills, increased creativity, higher self-esteem, improved problem-solving skills, and superior management of emotions.[2]

I wonder, can some children really be in contact with a person from the other side who is mentoring them?

I don't know, I'm asking.

All I am certain about is that the universe is a lot more complicated and mysterious than any scientist would have suggested when I was young.

Quantum teleportation alone is enough to convince me that our four-dimensional world (length, height, depth, and time) is a vast oversimplification.

If I understand correctly, quantum teleportation is the *state* of a particle transferring from one location to another without sending the particle itself. It was proven in 1997.[3]

Robin, there is a lot going on that we cannot fathom. Much that has always been labeled bogus or speculation could be true.

Your Friend Rick

---

1. "Children's Imaginary Friends: What to Know," *WebMD* website, Feb 15, 2024.

2. "Children's Imaginary Friends: What to Know," *WebMD* website, Feb 15, 2024.

3. "Is teleportation possible? Yes, in the quantum world," *U.S. National Science Foundation* website, July 6, 2020, and, "How Quantum teleportation Actually Works," *Popular Mechanics* website, Mar 16, 2017.

Doing Chores

Letter 8

———— ◆ ————

Dear Robin,

When we met in November of 1964, Samantha was 17 and I was 18. I immediately fell hard for her, and decade after decade the falling never stopped. Even now, Robin, every day I love her more.

Not once in all our 56 years of marriage did I wonder if I'd married the wrong person. I think this was because we both worked and still work, very hard at not taking each other for granted.

In day-to-day life, this translated into the fact that, almost always, no matter what I did, deep down it was for Samantha. Mowing the lawn, gapping the spark plugs, earning an income, repairing the refrigerator, washing the dishes, you name it. Rarely in the back of my mind was the thought, this is a chore and I dislike doing it. Usually, it was something like, Samantha will be pleased, or this will make Sam's life a bit better.

And she was pleased.

And she said so, in many ways.

In turn, when she did things that needed doing, her attitude was the same as mine. She did them for me because she loved me. (And still does.)

And I was pleased, and I said so, in many ways.

Very important: Doing for each other had a sort of ratcheting effect. Each spouse's appreciation reinforced the other's desire to please.

Robin, for some people this may seem improbable, but for us, it truly worked.

By the way, as I see it, the idea of "in turn" meaning in trade, is crucially important in marriage. It is another concept we will get into in the *Owner's Manual* so that it can become an automatic part of your day-to-day thinking.

In the *Owner's Manual*, we will explore many such concepts, hoping they become automatic habits. It may not seem like it while you are reading it, but it will pay off for you over and over for the rest of your life, I promise.

Your Friend Rick

Who Was Samantha?

Letter 9

———— ♦ ————

D ear Robin,

    You asked for more about Samantha.

You seem to be intrigued by her. You aren't the only one.

For starters, Sam could be breathtakingly charming.

She wanted to learn how to do a tune-up on our 1971 Volvo. Soon she was bent over the engine, growling in frustration, up to her elbows in dirt and grease, and using decidedly unladylike language on the spark plugs.

I asked her to promise something. Can't remember what it was. Not important.

She surprised me by standing straight up facing me, holding her oily hands against her temples with palms facing forward, and in a little girl voice declaring, "I double-whammy promise!"

I nearly fell down laughing.

She is unusual, no doubt. So unusual in fact that I will need several more letters to help you get to know her.

Here is one reason Sam was so successful in her careers: she never believed in equality.

If someone argued that women should strive for equality with men, Sam's response would be, why would I want to be dragged down to the level of men?

More new businesses are started by women than men,[1] and women who run their own businesses generate 10% more revenue in five years than men do.[2]

She never understood why a woman would get involved in politics. She was convinced politics is a dead-end street, almost certain to disappoint — almost certain to have costs greater than benefits.

Her attitude was always, if you want something, set your sights on that specific item, and go get it. Never let yourself be sidetracked into the political jungles where you will be suckered into the bottomless pit of corruption and failure.

She often mentioned my admonition that "political power corrupts the morals and the judgment."

When she was asked to attend political meetings, march in protests, solicit votes, or in other ways get political, she would shake her head at the colossal waste of time and energy.

Instead, after her stint as a public school teacher, which in those days paid deplorable wages, she adopted an ironclad rule.

She would never again work at a job that would pay less than she was worth.

While millions of women were spending their precious time and energy begging politicians to make them equal to men, Samantha was spending her time and energy working hard toward a Mercedes Benz, a backyard swimming pool, and luxury vacations.

Robin, Sam also derived a great deal of satisfaction from donating to battered women's shelters.

To hear the managers of the shelters tell it, she helped rescue a great many women who were in dire straits.

She had the money to do it. Because she earned it.

And she certainly helped many more people than she would have if entangled in the political jungles.

Again, after being a public school teacher, Samantha worked 45 years only at jobs that paid what she felt she was worth.

She's a modern example of the American rugged individualist, and this enabled her to enjoy the great satisfaction of helping others.

After all, who does not enjoy being a hero?

Your Friend Rick

P.S. Back to that double-whammy promise.

I cannot possibly tell you how much I love laughing with Sam.

As she grew older, she grew funnier, which made her increasingly charming and attractive.

I suspect the bit of magic she discovered is that being funny requires confidence, and to me, there is nothing more attractive than a woman who radiates confidence.

1. "Are Women-Owned Businesses as Successful as Male-Owned Businesses," *Score.org*, Sep 27, 2023.

2. "Harnessing the Power of Women-Owned Business," *Washington State University, Carson College of Business*, website, dated only 2024.

There Was a Day When Women Were Special

Letter 10

———— ♦ ————

D ear Robin,

Thanks again for writing. So good to hear from you!

You mentioned someone referring to a time when women were special.

You hit one of my hot buttons.

Born in 1887, my grandfather was the most influential person in my life.

He always wore a hat. When we walked down Main Street, he tipped it to any woman we passed.

In my early days of the 1940s and '50s, men would open doors for women. They'd help them with their chairs.

When in mixed groups, they'd expect women to walk down narrow corridors ahead of them.

If a group of men were talking "man talk" and a woman walked into the room, all the rough language came to a screeching halt. If one of the men did not comply, others would elbow him.

Everyone knew that if a man ever physically harmed his wife, he would be hunted down by her father, brothers, male cousins, and friends, and he would have a bad day.

In the 1970s and later, this specialness was labeled old-fashioned, and blown away. Political women said these courtesies were obsolete, they were ways of putting women down, of painting them as weak or even helpless.

Ridiculous. These were ways of acknowledging that women are superior. Especially morally superior.

But that specialness is all gone now. According to the National Domestic Violence Hotline, one in four women over age 18 is a victim of "severe physical violence by an intimate partner,"[1] and battered women's shelters cannot be built fast enough.

According to FBI statistics, each year there are more than a million cases of police arriving too late to prevent a murder, rape, or aggravated assault.[2]

That is a violent crime every three seconds.

If Sam is anything, it is a realist, and she decided she needed to do something to protect herself. So every two years she polished up her self-defense skills. Bringing herself back up to speed on legalities, safety, and marksmanship, she was trained as well or better than many police officers. The Sheriff's Department instructors called her Annie, after Annie Oakley. Carrying a Glock 26 equalizer, she never again walked in fear.

Robin, notice Sam did not wait for politics to make her equal. She made herself equal, and in my opinion even more than that.

By the way, she knew self-defense is less difficult than driving a car, but has much in common with it. Doing it badly is both easy and deadly. Doing it safely takes hours of repetitive training.

Your Friend Rick

P.S. I don't know anything about today's love songs, but going clear back into the 1800s, they were almost all about the woman's looks.

There was next to nothing about her character, her personality. Is she wonderfully ethical, logical, scientific, curious, farsighted, clever, and athletic?

We never know. All we find out is she's a looker.

To me, probably the most captivating thing about Sam is that she is interesting. She never stops teaching me things.

---

1. *Thehotline.org* Supported by the Department of Health and Human Services.

2. *FBI* website, Violent Crime.

Samantha's Interests

Letter 11

———— ✦ ————

Dear Robin,

You are right, Sam's personality is remarkable, no doubt. Those who knew her, often talk about her uniqueness. She had numerous interests.

She enjoyed baking, and early in our marriage had a sewing machine and made her own clothes.

She insisted I teach her how to work on cars. In those days, the sixties, a woman working on cars was unheard of.

In her teens she enjoyed playing tennis, and in her twenties, volleyball and touch football.

She loves art, especially the Dutch Masters and Impressionists. One day when writing these letters to you, I took a time out for us to visit an art festival. She sees through my eyes and hears through my ears, and she loves it.

Years ago when traveling to foreign cities, our usual routine for visiting museums was for us to have breakfast together, then split up. She would go to art museums, and me to history museums.

We'd meet for lunch, then continue on our separate ways. At dinner, we'd teach each other about our most interesting discoveries.

Sam also loves science and science fiction, especially the many possibilities and insights raised by Gene Roddenberry's Star Trek series.

She collected rocks. To her, a day wading in a creek bed or roaming a beach in search of unique specimens was a thrill. Especially in spring, when the wildflowers were in bloom.

Christmas is her absolute most fun time of year. All year long, one of her treasured hobbies was hand-sewing detailed fabric Christmas ornaments. We spent many an evening sitting closely side-by-side in front of the fire and TV, while she stitched red, green, and white works of art for the tree.

There are 53 of those ornaments. Most are the size of ordinary tree ornaments, but twelve are much larger and more detailed. One is four feet across. I'm not kidding, Robin, four feet. One stitch at a time.

And all are done meticulously, and flawlessly. I'm so proud of her!

Speaking of the fire, in winter we often spent part of the evenings sitting on the sofa in each other's arms watching TV in front of the fire. We had the furniture arranged so that we'd be directly under a knot in the natural wood ceiling. The knot was shaped like a heart.

She loved hearts. Some of her most fun times were walking along a beach searching for heart-shaped stones.

She'd bring them home and scatter them around the house because they were so meaningful to her.

Speaking of the ocean, in our early years Sam loved to eat salads and fish. But she gave up the fish after she became an avid snorkel diver and got to know some of the tropical ones, especially the colorful but shy and slow varieties of boxfish.

Her favorite sea creatures are turtles. They took a liking to her. On the "Big Island" of Hawaii, we had a favorite small beach where we waded into the water. Two turtles would swim up to her, one on each side, and escort her out to the reef.

For music, her favorite singers are The Kingston Trio, Barbra Streisand, and Helen Reddy. Perhaps her favorite song is Reddy's "I Am Woman."

For her final 20 years of life on this planet, our song was "I'll Never Find Another You," by The Seekers; 1964. It describes us perfectly. I hope you will listen to it. As I write this, it's on YouTube.

And while you are at it, please listen to the 1957 song "Wonderful, Wonderful" by Johnny Mathis. Word for word, Mathis describes what was a typical day for Samantha and me whenever we were at our seaside home.

We did it regularly almost until the day she crossed over.

It was made possible by the marital practices I will explain to you later in these letters. I hope you and your spouse find delights as wonderful and savor them often.

Your Friend Rick

More About Samantha

Letter 12

———— ◆ ————

Dear Robin,

For eight years, Samantha was a public school teacher, grades kindergarten through sixth. It was the toughest job she ever had, by far; the emotional strain was crushing. She not only taught the children, she empathized with them, so she often came home an emotional wreck. Not all children have wise and ethical parents.

Good teachers are heroes, no doubt about it.

Later Sam became a highly successful sales manager for a Fortune 500 corporation, then the marketing manager for Henry Madison Research, and editor of our *Early Warning Report* (EWR).

It was largely Sam's business skills that were responsible for the resounding success of EWR. She insisted that our publication be wide-ranging and unique, giving the readers insights and guidance they could not get anywhere else.

At a time when a typical financial newsletter was a success if its subscription renewal rate was 25%, ours was a legend in the industry at 90%. This was largely due to Samantha's marketing, skillfully using the advertising to describe the content.

In the mid-1950s when I was about ten years old, I had an older cousin named Judy, who was the first girl in our clan to attend college.

Judy could win a debate with any of the men.

Eight years later, listening to Samantha was like listening to Judy.

Decades after that, Sam was regarded as a sage. Friends and acquaintances routinely approached her asking for advice.

She was a tad taller than most women of her generation, and athletic, a lifeguard. This gave her an imposing physical stature that reinforced her credibility. When she walked into a room, heads turned.

Sam oozed confidence from every pore. But in her world, everyone was treated with respect. In her eyes, plumbers, mechanics, farm workers, and anyone else who got their hands dirty, were special — above architects, engineers, and surgeons. She'd say, "Imagine our lives without them."

But no one was ever treated as well as her dogs. Truth be known, Sam may have been the person who inspired the bumper sticker, "The more I know people, the better I like my dog."

Your Friend Rick

P.S. I hope these last few letters have given you a taste of why I love Samantha so completely. There's a lot to love. If I had to pick just one word to describe her, it would be depth.

P.P.S. What about me? How should I be described?

My best friend refers to me as, the ever-optimistic curmudgeon.

Samantha's Failings

Letter 13

———— ◆ ————

Dear Robin,

I do not mean to paint Samantha as some kind of superwoman. As a teacher and a sales manager, she ran herself into the ground. She was both success-driven and help-driven, which is a grueling combination.

In other words, Robin, Sam was all engine and no brakes, and it wore her down.

She was also terrible about training her dogs. If I hadn't done it, it would never have gotten done. She was just too soft-hearted. She could be tough with me, or any other human, but couldn't bring herself to be that way with a dog.

She also stayed loyal to many people who treated her badly. She was almost masochistic in that way.

For me, Sam's most annoying failing was clutter. She wanted to save uncountable items. She realized governments are hell-bent on wrecking the world economy, and she was afraid we would run out of important stuff. But there wasn't room to store it all.

So, Sam was far from perfect. But who isn't?

Besides, where it counted most, being a wife, I cannot imagine anyone being better at it. When I think of how bound and determined she was to make our old-fashioned marriage a success, I cry.

Your Friend Rick

Six Words of Warning

Letter 14

———— ◆ ————

Dear Robin

One day Samantha and I were having lunch with several friends. As usual, she slipped into the booth first, and I began to follow so that we could hold hands. We always held hands under the table or across it.

But someone else began to slide in ahead of me.

I said nothing but my expression thundered.

Then someone observed, "Never get between Rick and Sam."

I often think of that incident. If I had to boil our whole 56 years of marriage down into one sentence, it might be those six words.

It took years for their importance to sink in, and to make sure everyone obeyed them in every way. But once we drew that line, we never let anyone cross it.

Your Friend Rick

Notes

Book One – Part 2

Getting to Know Love

Better Ways to Say
I Love You

Letter 15

————— ✦ —————

D ear Robin,

You asked for ideas on better ways to say "I love you."

In my opinion, I love you has become terribly overused. I love my wife, but I also love walks on the beach, science fiction, and chocolate chip cookies.

In fact, love is so overused it can sound like a throw-away line or an afterthought.

Oh, by the way, "I love you."

Here, Robin, are some alternatives. You might consider using these or others often. Some are cliches, but so what! It's the thought that counts.

- "I adore you with all my heart."

- "You are my everything."

- "I am committed to you forever."

- "I love you to Andromeda and back." (Sam's favorite, said to me almost daily.)

- "You make my heart sing."

- "You are the wind beneath my wings."

- "You mean the world to me."

- "You make me ecstatic."

- "You are my soulmate."

- "You are my world."

- "I will love you forever."

- "I crave you even more than chocolate."

- "I love you sooooo much!"

- "Without you I'd be 10% of what I am."

- "You are the love of my life."

- "You mean so much to me."

- "I cherish you."

- "I treasure you."

- "I relish you."

- "When I look at you, I'm all in."

- "You are my life." (My favorite, often said to her.)

At one time or another, we used almost all of these. I wish we'd used them more. You might want to make your own personal list, too. The extra effort may impress.

Your Friend Rick

P.S. Robin, perhaps a good test of the health of your marriage is, does this "mushy" kind of talk feel genuine to you?

Samantha's Astonishing Story

Letter 16

———— ✦ ————

Dear Robin,

Again, if you are convinced there is no hereafter you might want to skip the following several pages. Slightly altered, they are from the March 2024 issue of our newsletter.

Many thanks to subscriber JMP for reminding me that folks have been asking to hear more about the experiences Samantha and I have been having since her passing on September 3rd.

We never dreamed anything like this could be possible. Here are some main points.

Sam was born in 1947, me in 1946. In our 30s and 40s, we had no spiritual beliefs.

In the 1990s, we became captivated by the concept of spirituality. This was due to our amazing experiences at Stonehenge and numerous European churches, as well as at the Colosseum in Rome, plus our friendship

with renowned anthropologist Hank Wesselman who specialized in the mysteries of "primitive" spirituality.

In the spring of 2023, Samantha was having occasional mild abdominal pain, which we ignored. Then it grew worse. Testing and imaging began, although her pain was still not severe. The testing and imaging were sparking some anxiety which again is not unusual in such cases.

The evening of July 30th we were snuggling side by side, holding hands, and watching TV, which was our end-of-day custom. Suddenly I noticed Sam was highly agitated.

I asked, "What's happening?" She said she had become "Upset, nervous, afraid" but did not know why. At this time no one had suspicions of cancer. The doctors were focused on a herniated navel, which we understood to be a mechanical problem, not a disease.

I suggested Sam write out some notes describing what she was experiencing. These notes became the main source for this article.

About 25 years earlier, Sam had developed a friendship with what she calls her "spirits and angels." She talked with them perhaps weekly.

The evening of July 30th, "a huge number of spirits and angels" appeared to her (but not to me, I've never seen them). They told her they were "Here to help," and they caressed her arms, legs, and head. "It was a wonderful feeling and I just sat back and enjoyed it," she wrote.

Then they told her something serious was headed her way but they would be with her "24 hours a day" all the way, so she could "remain calm."

On August 31st we met with a six-person surgical team and received the crushing news that she had cancer and it had gone too far. There was nothing anyone could do.

Until that meeting, we thought we had a rough time ahead of us but we would overcome it just like we'd overcome every other obstacle in our 56-year marriage. We would have decades more together, we thought.

The oncologists said we might have one or two months.

It turned out to be four days.

After Samantha's passing, I heard...

...nothing from her for perhaps three weeks. Then I began sometimes catching a brief whisper of a word here and there, too faint to understand.

As the weeks went by, she developed the ability to whisper more clearly. The first words I could make out were, "I love you."

She has told me, the other side where she now resides is much nicer than here. No wars, no government or other criminal activity, and the surrounding territory is breathtakingly beautiful.

She says it is all lovely, much like a Swiss Alps valley in summer.

Samantha's joy at her surroundings makes me wonder, do humans like to visit natural places such as

Yosemite, Hawaii, and the Painted Desert because there they taste the other side?

And, regarding the other side, I asked her, how magnificent is it?

She said a good comparison is that where you and I are — this reality — is at the bottom of the nearly barren Lake Tahoe, and where she is, is the Great Barrier Reef.

Sam tells me that in transitioning from the here to the hereafter, some memories are lost. So she tells me that in the part of the hereafter she is experiencing, there is an adaption period — I call it boot camp — which is no fun. But other spirits are assigned as mentors, and adaptive skills are gradually mastered.

What other areas of the hereafter may be like, she doesn't know.

Samantha's primary instructor is my Uncle Bill, of whom I greatly approve. He was always a fine, gentle person who cared about her greatly.

All this comes as a tremendous shock to Samantha and me. Call us naïve, but we'd never thought about what the other side might be. We were so baffled by wondering, would sitting on a cloud playing a harp for all eternity be heaven or hell?, that we never went further. We had simply experienced enough strange events to conclude a hereafter of some kind is fact, and we blithely walked by the question of what exactly it is.

I cannot prove any of this. But Sam and I have encountered enough strange events which, for want of a better word, we call spiritual, that for perhaps 30 years the hereafter has been as real to us as the here, even though we did not know what it was.

Anthropologist Hank Wesselman told us most so-called primitive cultures, like those in the Amazon or New Guinea, who are not suffocating in technological distractions, experience spiritual incidents often and take them for granted; they're just a normal part of life.

Perhaps the main takeaway…

…in all this is that the "spirits and angels" who promised to stay with Sam and help her, showed up July 30th, a month *before* anyone suspected something horrific was approaching.

As a professional skeptic, I fully understand someone seeing our story as wishful thinking or imagination — a coping mechanism — on my part. But I have her notes, in her handwriting. I believe the July 30th warning from Sam's spirits and angels is strong enough evidence of a hereafter it would convince even Sherlock Holmes.

I am sure now that the real you is not your body but your spirit, and it does not die. After all, when we humans fall in love, is it with our mates' bones and muscles, or with their souls?

By the way. I have long believed many couples who have been together for decades develop a sort of "connection through the ether" which enables them to occasionally read each other's minds.

Sam tells me I'm right about that, and reckons that when we were together on this side, we were effectively connected about 20%. Now she estimates 90%, and her soul is situated in my solar plexus.

Never knew anything about the solar plexus until she referred to it. Looked it up. It's the site of a great deal of the body's electrical activity.

Why don't many people experience this?

I think it's likely they do. A person who has passed does try to connect with loved ones but has not yet learned the necessary skills.

The loved ones might detect some kind of murmur or vibe, as the loved one practices, but can't make it out. They soon dismiss the sensation, forget it, and move on, never trying to help nurture it.

If you suspect this may be the case in your own life — if you would like to make a spiritual connection with a loved one — I suggest you go to work on it and keep at it. I am no expert on such things, but I might suggest talking to the person often, in quiet without any distractions. Tell them you want to talk to them, then do so at least every day.

I don't know if it will work for you but give it a try.

That's Samantha's story so far

She tells me persons in boot camp do not experience much of the other side until they are adapted and can safely be out on their own.

Maybe I'm crazy, but if so, crazy is working for me.

As for Samantha and me now, we continue our daily custom of sitting on the veranda watching the sunset and discussing the day's events.

Your Friend Rick

P.S. You might be interested in the article "Does an Afterlife Obviously Exist?" by Jens Amberts, *Psychology Today* website, Apr 29, 2022. It's an eye-opener.

Removing Photos

Letter 17

————— ♦ —————

Dear Robin,

Perhaps a month after Samantha's passing I realized that each time I glanced at one of the many photos of her around our house I was overwhelmed with grief. Robin, sometimes the photos hit me so hard I was suddenly down on the floor curled up and crying like a child.

The repeated attacks of sadness were ruining what was left of my life.

This I can tell you with great confidence: living with Samantha, and observations of other marriages, convinced me men need women far more than women need men.

I reasoned, I am continually being ambushed by my memories; I need to do something about the triggers.

After giving it a lot of thought, I realized, as mentioned in a previous letter, that when we humans fall in love, it is not with our mates' bones and muscles, it's with their spirit.

The spirit is the personality.

Her face and body are gone. But what I love so much, her personality, is still here.

Robin, she has not departed, she has only transitioned. We now converse at least twice per day.

Expecting to stay deeply in love with Samantha forever, I realized her pictures were no longer her.

They also caused me to be backward-looking.

I need to be forward-looking, to build a new life in which I remain profoundly in love with Sam, because the real Sam, her personality, is still with me.

I gathered up all but three small photos, placing them in a drawer for safekeeping.

It's been perhaps five months since I did that, and now when I think of Sam, I see her face and body less and feel her presence, her charm, charisma, and magnetism more.

In other words, Sam's body is past tense, but her spirit is definitely here. That's what this book is about. Samantha is here, and she and I are working together as a team, to help you and others develop the warm, close, old-fashioned connection we had *and still have.*

By the way, Sam came from a family where it was practically holy writ that men are superior to women, and the men never missed a chance to put the women down. So I watched diligently for opportunities to help Sam feel good about herself. My favorite T-shirt says, "I ASKED GOD TO MAKE ME A BETTER MAN. HE SENT ME MY WIFE."

A couple of months ago I bought a dozen of those shirts in different sizes to give to my male friends. If there is anything better for a marriage than helping a wife feel good about herself, I don't know what it could be.

Your Friend Rick

P.S. Robin, please bear in mind that when I speak highly of old-fashioned love, I am not claiming everything old-fashioned was better. Much was not. But a wise couple will pick and choose. They will revive and use whatever works well for them.

After all, look at the state of marriage today, especially the trivialization of sex. Plus the divorce rate, and the filled-to-over-flowing battered women's shelters.

There are animals that mate for life. But when it comes to the promise of till-death-do-us-part, the typical human today isn't even doing it as well as coyotes do.

Teamwork

Letter 18

———— ◆ ————

D ear Robin,

One of the best things Samantha and I ever did for our marriage was start a business together. It's called Henry Madison Research.

Growing out of our considerable business and military experience, our newsletter helps investors cope with the economic, political, and geopolitical insanity that seems to get worse year by year as governments gradually undermine everything good.

We found that one of the wonderful surprises of building and running a partnership is, by following the guidelines in the *Owner's Manual*. Earning money together not only strengthened the bond between us, it was exciting and even erotic.

Which brings to mind one of Sam's favorite jokes.

When we were a start-up, she would sometimes answer the phone to chat with the customers and ask how we were doing and what we could do better.

Some callers would ask her if she knew me or ever saw me.

To our assistants, she would joke that someday she was going to say, "Oh yes, I just passed him in the hallway, and this is my night to sleep with him."

Your Friend Rick

Our Love Did Not Stop

Letter 19

———— ♦ ————

D ear Robin,

One afternoon during the writing of these letters, about six months after Sam had passed, she and I were talking, and for the millionth time in our marriage, I told her it was impossible for me to describe how much I love her.

She stunned me by coming back with, "I'm glad. I still *need* you to love me."

I said, "But you're on the other side. How can you need anything? How can you feel what you felt here?"

She replied, "I don't know. All I know is I still need your love. I crave it, as much as I ever did."

I had always assumed that once a person went to the other side, their needs stopped.

"Are there other things you require?" I asked.

"None I know of. Certainly not food, water, or other animal necessities. Just your love."

Notice, Robin, love is surely an animal characteristic. It has biochemical components. All three of our dogs loved us, and we loved them.

But it apparently has spiritual ones, too, and the spiritual ones carry on in the hereafter.

More and more, I suspect the spiritual facets of what happens between lovers are as profound as they are mysterious.

Your Friend Rick

P.S. In interviews and public appearances, I have often been asked how to become a successful writer.

I always answer, "It's quite simple. All you need do is find a woman who loves you so much she will subsidize you for twenty years even though she thinks you're crazy, and then one day you're rich!"

I Memorized Her

Letter 20

————— ◆ —————

Dear Robin,

One of the best things I ever did was force the development of a habit.

I would often remind myself that Samantha and I would probably not depart at the same time. The day would likely come when one of us would still be here and the other would not.

So I carefully memorized her. Day after day, I would take mental videos of Sam — sometimes cooking, other times gathering roses for the living room, showering, swimming, driving, shopping, you name it.

Now I have a head full of these simple everyday videos, and I play them over and over.

Your Friend Rick

Her Voice

Letter 21

————— ✦ —————

Dear Robin,

I miss her voice so much. We talk every day at least twice for 20 minutes or so, but it is not yet the same as when she was on this side. She still has not learned to make more than a strong whisper, although it gets clearer by the month. And, she can comfortably say full sentences now.

When Samantha was on this side, she never talked just to be talking. Each sentence had a purpose, a meaning, often to teach me something.

To me, her voice was like music, although her singing voice was even worse than mine. But I loved hearing it. It meant she was near.

Today I would give anything just to hear her read from the white pages of the phone book. I am not kidding.

(Sam, I miss you so much, but I'm also thrilled to know you are there waiting for me. I've saved seven phone books to bring with me.)

Your Friend Rick

Notes

Book One – Part 3

Differences Between Men & Women

We Banished That Awful Word

Letter 22

————— ✦ —————

Dear Robin,

Love is wonderful and essential.

So are romance and sex.

But the three are not the same, which we will get into shortly.

By the way, one of the most helpful things Samantha and I ever did was banish the word sex from our marriage.

We didn't have sex. Sex is what happens in a barnyard.

We had affection, romance, gentleness, security, rapport, lovemaking, caressing, connection, caring, and most of all intimacy.

Robin, that is our magic word, intimacy. One reason we like it is, that it prevents trivialization.

Intimacy is a lot more than just a "normal bodily function," as sex now is often regarded to be. Intimacy is a serious and *essential* blessing, perhaps even a miracle.

More on that shortly.

Sex can be taken lightly. Intimacy is deep-rooted and profound.

But there is something even more serious, essential, and perhaps even miraculous, which we will explore in great detail in Book Two, the *Owner's Manual*.

These days it is almost completely unknown, but by the time you get to my last letter, you will be highly proficient at it, and will be greatly admired for this, I promise.

By the way, I am only lightly covering many of the usual topics you may have studied in other books about marriage.

Communication, respect, frankness, politeness, etc. These and much more are important, no doubt, but all of them together are not as crucial as the one to which all of the *Owner's Manual* is devoted, and which these days practically no one talks about. Or even knows about.

But first, Robin, we need to lay more groundwork, which is found in human DNA.[1]

Hang on to your hat, this will be a wild ride.

Your Friend Rick

P.S. Our marriage was so remarkably close and warm that word about us got around.

A few days after Samantha's passing, I had a total stranger walk up to me on the street to offer condolences and remark on how much she admired our closeness.

P.P.S. You might want to hold off implementing some of my suggestions until your spouse has read about them.

An unexplained change in behavior can be worrisome even when it is a good one.

---

1. DNA. The molecule that is the carrier of the genetic information of nearly all living organisms including humans.

Intimacy

Letter 23

———— ♦ ————

Dear Robin,

It's practically a mandatory ritual of every guy's life. A mixed group of younger and older males are standing around gabbing, and the subject rolls around to what it always does, women.

One of the young guys blurts out, "It must be great to be married and have all the sex you want!"

The older ones fall down laughing.

Men are from the planet Testosterone, and women are from its neighbor Estrogen.

Testosterone is the main sex hormone. Men have a lot, and women not so much. In fact, men have between ten and twenty *times* as much as women.[1]

Robin, in the Stone Age, testosterone was much more essential than it is now. When it came time to fight off a sabertooth tiger, the tribe, armed with nothing but rocks, sticks, and courage, needed a platoon of hyped-up young males willing to fight to the death.

Today's males therefore have the biochemistry for lethal combat, but there are not many sabertooth tigers on which to expend their energies.

My suggestion on this is in two parts. First, talk about it — both of you. Get your feelings out in the open.

Second, stop thinking sex and start thinking *intimacy*.

In Samantha's and my opinion, the physical act, which can be disappointingly brief, especially for the lady, should be seen as just the launch for the intimacy, which might continue for hours. Or even days.

One of our favorite memories, Robin, is of making love in a farmhouse in the Swiss Alps. After the hot-and-heavy, we luxuriated in each other's arms, gazing out the farmhouse window at the snow-capped Eiger, Monch, and Jungfrau peaks.

We often reminisce about that, and sometimes relived parts at home in the hot tub, under the supervision of our dogs, who never objected.

Your Friend Rick

---

1. "All About Testosterone in Women," *Healthline* website, June 10, 2019.

An Old-Fashioned Idea

Letter 24

———— ✦ ————

D ear Robin,

The sexual revolution trivialized sex. Something that was once possibly the most powerful glue that holds a marriage together became just a game, a sport, an athletic event.

But sex is so powerful it can overwhelm and dominate everything else.

Including love.

Here is a question that is old but as valid today as a hundred years ago: Are you in love, or just in lust?

Robin, if I were not married and met a woman I considered a possible marriage partner, I might send her a handwritten letter or card saying something like this:

"You are wonderfully interesting to me — smart, funny, clever, and beautiful.

*I have long been lonely and in search of a lifetime partner. But I do not want our relationship to be about sex; I want it to be about love. To me, overwhelming though it can be, sex is something to get around to, not something that controls us. **It is not a goal.***

So I would like to have, what is these days, an unusual old-fashioned love affair. If we are lucky enough to have one that grows to the point we wind up at the altar, we will not see each other with our clothes off or join each other in bed until our honeymoon.

That way, dear, the development of our love can be more easily controlled by our emotions, not our hormones."

Your Friend Rick

P.S. Some good news for a change! A rigorous sexual-content study by film data analyst Stephen Follows examined the 250 highest-grossing theater movies in the US since 2000.

The study found that in 2000, less than 20% of movies were without sexual content. But by 2023, this had become almost half.[1]

This fits with studies showing that Generation Z (born 1997-2012) is having less sex.[2]

I wonder. Have the young begun figuring out that the boomers' anything-goes "sexual revolution" led later generations down the garden path to hurt and loneliness?

---

1. "Frisky Business," *The Economist* magazine, May 4, 2024, p.73,

2. "5 Big Sex Issues Gen Z-ers Bring Up In Therapy All The Time," *Huffpost.com*, Mar 22, 2024.

But I Don't Have Time

Letter 25

———— ✦ ————

Dear Robin,

You might be saying, "But I am terribly busy." My job, housework, cooking, car washing, exercise, lawn watering, and the list goes on and on.

What if I don't have time to implement your suggestions to help my marriage?

Three words: *prioritize, delegate, discard.*

First, make a list of all the things in your life that are important to you. Then arrange them in order, most important to least.

Second, Robin, identify the ones you can delegate to others, or hire out to others to do for you.

Third, work your way through the remaining list, and discard items of the smallest importance.

Put your marriage at the top of the list, and review the list monthly. Schedule these reviews on your calendar.

Your Friend Rick

Stay Clean

Letter 26

———— ✦ ————

D ear Robin,

As I think most women see it, to remain attractive to your mate, there is hardly anything as important as cleanliness.

Especially if you are the guy. I am sure there are women who are exceptions, but in general, I think women are much more sensitive to dirt and stink than men are.

Robin, let's face it. A man has so much testosterone in him that when it comes to romance, he could probably manage to ignore the odor of a buffalo.

Also, a woman's sense of smell is more acute than a man's, and I am sure this heightens the importance of the man's need to look, smell, and be clean.

And well-groomed. People who make TV commercials are experts at knowing what women want a man to look like. Study those guys. Do they look shabby to you?

In my opinion, never expect to be invited to her side of the bed unless you are practically immaculate. Of course, she might invite you, but why lower your chances?

On the other hand, I'm not a woman. What do I know?

Your Friend Rick

Is He Listening to You?

Letter 27

————— ◆ —————

Dear Robin,

When Samantha and I were first married, I heard continual complaints about me not listening to her.

"We don't have enough gas in the car to get to the gas station! Why didn't you get gas? I told you three times to get gas!"

Or, "Why didn't you take the trash cans out? I told you four times the cans should go out!"

Or, "I told you five times to pick me up and take me to my emergency dentist appointment at 4:00 pm! What, do I need to threaten you with divorce to get you to listen?"

My reply, Robin, was usually something like, "What? What? I don't remember you telling me anything about that."

Is it truc I had been ignoring her?

No.

Is it true I did not hear her?

Yes. Absolutely. Guilty as charged.

Not hearing, and ignoring, are not the same thing.

I eventually developed a theory on yet another of the many differences between men and women.

But let's stop right here for a moment.

Among some political groups these days it is fashionable to believe that men and women are the same and should be treated the same.

I have already tipped my hand on that. I am not of that persuasion. Call me a Neanderthal, but it is my opinion that men and women are different.

Here's the story.

As soon as my testosterone began to gush, probably around age 3^1, I began making a careful study of women. I eventually realized that, yes indeed they really are not the same.

I don't know when I developed my theory of how their brains are different, probably about age 35. Too late to avoid a lot of heated words.

My theory:

A woman's brain is designed to juggle a dozen oranges, and if you hand her a 13th orange, she can handle that, too, and maybe even a 14th.

A man's brain is designed to hold one watermelon, and if you hand him an orange he'll drop his watermelon.

So men hang on to their watermelons tightly.

Samantha really did remind me to do things all those times. But she didn't have my attention.

One way a wife can handle this, Robin, is to keep a length of two-by-four handy, and before you tell him something important, smack him with it so that you know he's noticed you.[2]

A better way is to simply touch him, on the wrist, shoulder, or somewhere more intimate, squeeze gently, look him in the eye, and say, "I have something to tell you, are you listening?"

When he says, "Uh huh," don't believe him. Wait.

When he finally breaks out of his concentration — when you are sure he's dropped his watermelon — then you can tell him.

Your Friend Rick

"The average woman would rather have beauty than brains because the average man can see better than he can think." — Mark Twain

P.S. Studies show men can multitask as well as women, but multitasking is not what I was talking about. The topics were concentration and distraction. I think women and men are different.

---

1. That's a joke.

2. Just kidding.

Our Paleolithic Programming

Letter 28

————— ♦ —————

D ear Robin,

I am not a scientist but I know a little about paleontology and more about economic history.

In my writing, I often refer to the fact that our minds are from the 20th and 21st centuries, but our bodies and brains are from the Paleolithic or the Old Stone Age. (As opposed to the Mesolithic and Neolithic — Middle Stone Age and New Stone Age.)

With a background in economic history, I have become convinced that a significant part of our DNA was programmed into us by the economic conditions of the Paleolithic.

This programming influences much of what goes on in a marriage today.

Here is perhaps the most important Paleolithic fact of life: A man can produce scores or even hundreds of children per year, but a woman only one or sometimes twins or triplets.

Therefore, Robin, men are vastly more expendable than women, which was fortunate because of the sabertooth tiger problem.

Which leads to the testosterone problem. Next letter.

Your Friend Rick

Beware of Testosterone Poisoning

Letter 29

———— ◆ ————

D ear Robin,

When a sabertooth tiger comes into the village, who would you send to fight it off? We don't know.

All the sabertooth tigers are gone, and scientific evidence about this problem is sparse or nonexistent.

But we do have logic. Would the people sent to fight the tiger be female? No. Absolutely not.

Women are not expendable. Men are. The people sent to die are males, especially young ones.

You would not send the older ones. They and the older women are the tribe's most valuable treasures.

In a time before writing, they were the storehouses of experience, knowledge, and wisdom. Without old people, everybody dies.

As the tiger approached, we can imagine what the strategizing was like. The older and wiser men would say, "We sure would like to go out to fight the tiger like you young whippersnappers. We wish we could be heroes like you. But fighting tigers is a team effort, and we're over the hill now; we might let you down. You'll be better off if we just hang back and comfort the women."

Robin, we can logically assume the young males who survived were those who were strongest and fastest, which means the ones with the most testosterone.

Therefore, women today must cope with hundreds of thousands of years of nature selecting for males with heavy loads of that substance.

I think this accounts for wars, crime, bar fights, street gangs, and politics.

I call it testosterone poisoning.

Here is what it all boils down to. The typical modern male comes standard equipped with enough testosterone to take on and kill a sabertooth tiger using only stones, pointed sticks, and coarse language.[1]

But there are no longer any sabertooth tigers. Therefore, to my mind, the number one job of a wife is to civilize her husband. The sooner both realize it, the better off both will be.

A marriage is likely to be much more enjoyable if both parties help each other with this terribly frustrating challenge.

Robin, what may work is to agree that when she observes what might be symptoms of the poisoning, she whispers in his ear, "Too much testosterone?" And he answers, "Thank you."

If that does not work, I think in most cases she has no choice but to whisper, "If you don't cool it you ain't gittin' any."

It's not something a person swimming in testosterone wants to hear, but I cannot think of anything more likely to work. Maybe you can. But I hope you don't need to.

Your Friend Rick

P.S. Have you ever walked down a dark street at night and found yourself being followed by a group of young males? How did you feel?

This isn't to say testosterone is evil, just that **the human male is designed for a world that no longer exists**.

The sooner he and his mate accept this, and act to counter it, the happier both will be. The system of thinking we will explore in the *Owner's Manual* will be a great help.

Also, I am not saying women are without Paleolithic programming. It seems likely to me they have some. Maybe a lot. But not being a woman, I doubt I am qualified to say much about it. Although I probably will.

Actor Charlton Heston once said to me, "When a man marries, he is taking on a lover. When a woman marries, she is taking on a project."

---

1. The Paleolithic, or Old Stone Age, was about 2.5 million to 12,000 years ago. The bow and arrow was not likely invented till roughly 65,000 years ago.

More About Dealing With Testosterone Poisoning

Letter 30

———— ✦ ————

Dear Robin,

Whenever you are in the company of a "nice guy" — and yes, there are some — you are meeting one who has himself under control. One way males achieve this is by directing their energies into Stone Age behaviors that are still useful.

I have long been an avid collector of emergency supplies and equipment and am absolutely devastating with a 12-gauge pump shotgun.

But not because Samantha was helpless. Far from it. There has rarely been a woman who could protect herself as well as Samantha. Her athletic body was strong, and as I said earlier, her self-defense trainers called her Annie Oakley.

My favorite feminist hero, Annie Oakley (1860-1926) was astoundingly adept. In demonstrations before audiences, at 30 paces she could split a playing card edge-on, and hit dimes tossed into the air. Again, at 30 paces.

I am sure my obsession with protecting Sam is in my DNA.

And the flip side of it is in hers. Capable as a modern woman can be, her body and brain remain, like those of us men, Stone Age. Despite the fact that the equalizer — the handgun — has been invented, I think a woman needs to *see and hear* with her own eyes and ears that her male is ready and able to protect her on the physical level.

Sports can not only keep a man healthy, they can demonstrate physical prowess.

Also, Sam enjoyed a warm, fuzzy feeling when I would make a comment such as, "I'll keep an eye on that guy, he looks suspicious," or something else that reminded her I had her back.

A favorite song of ours, Robin, is Ella Fitzgerald's, "Someone To Watch Over Me."

In my next letter, more about the testosterone problem.

Your Friend Rick

Testosterone Poisoning in the Bedroom

Letter 31

Dear Robin,

It is no secret that the mere sight of a woman's body can stimulate the male. Indeed, the mere sight of parts — meaning hints — can do it.

My mother often said, "A woman's best asset is a man's imagination."

I have read studies that show the signs of beauty and health are the same.

Given what the Stone Age economy was like, this should not be surprising.

Right up until the takeoff of industrial capitalism around 1776, life was unimaginably awful.

In the words of English philosopher Thomas Hobbes, life was "solitary, poor, nasty, brutish and short."

Anyone who lived past 20 was lucky. Most died in childhood.[1]

Winter brought the threat of freezing and disease, and spring often brought starvation. Robin, imagine trying to feel amorous when you haven't eaten in a week.

Few diseases had cures.

Until industrial capitalism, there were no toothbrushes or toothpaste, much less dentists. Tooth decay was so awful people commonly died of it.

In fact, death from tooth decay was a constant threat until the 20th century; Samantha's grandmother died of it.

Try to imagine kissing someone who has a mouth full of rotten teeth.

As far as we know, the use of fire was not known till about 400,000 BC. What male could perform when he has hypothermia and frostbite?

There were no bathtubs, showers, or soap, much less hot water.

Yet the males were able to do it, at least well enough to produce children.

Imagine how much testosterone it took to accomplish that. Should we measure it in pounds or gallons?

Well, males today inherited that much and, being so much healthier thanks to industrial capitalism, perhaps a lot more.

Robin, please pause and think about it for a moment.

The healthy modern male may have even more testosterone than his Paleolithic ancestors, and those ancestors had enough to charge a sabertooth tiger armed with little more than courage.

There is a good side and a bad side to this.

The good side is that whenever a woman feels in the mood, her mate is ready.

The bad side is, when she is not in the mood, he's ready.

What to do about it?

I think you need to talk to each other.

Next letter.

Your Friend Rick

P.S. My explaining the testosterone problem is in no way meant to let uncivilized males off the hook for their horrible behavior.

But how many can solve the problem if they don't know they have it?

Today it is not as big a secret as it was when I was young.

The very idea that a man had hormones would have brought laughs. Everyone "knew" only women had hormones.

Even today, as far as I know, a male's hormones are not widely discussed or understood.

I simply cannot imagine a group of males sitting around a poker table with beer and pretzels discussing their hormone problems.

Women talk about their hormones a lot, and in big groups, whole auditoriums full. But men? I've never, ever seen it.

But there is this. Males my age spend a lot of time shaking their heads in exasperation as they observe the behaviors of the young ones.

Sometimes it seems the young ones are bound and determined to turn their lives into dumpster fires.

---

1. "Mortality in the past: every second child died," *Our World in Data* website, by Max Roser, Apr 11, 2023.

Ladies, It's a His & Hers Problem

Letter 32

———— ♦ ————

D ear Robin,

The awful truth is that guys are in the grip of that despicable Stone Age hormone, and lovers must find a way to cope with it.

Notice I wrote lovers, plural.

Robin, this isn't just a his problem, it's also a hers problem. She agreed to live with the tiger killer. So I believe she should start by *talking* about it with him.

Try making this observation a topic of discussion: I once heard a doctor say "The only time a woman knows what it is like to be a man is in the ten minutes before she has an orgasm. And the only time a man knows what it is like to be a woman is in the ten minutes after he's had an orgasm."

When I point this out, men usually say "yep," and women often blurt out "Ohmygod I never realized!"

If you really love each other and want a long-term loving bond, then the two of you together *must* find a way to handle this biochemical problem nature dumped onto you.

You can't cure it, but you can manage it, as I shall suggest shortly.

By the way, this is not to say biochemical problems do not bother women. In my opinion, any guy who does not acknowledge that women do suffer, and offer to help in whatever ways he can, is poor husband material.

She does not choose her hormonal problems any more than we choose ours, and I have known many women who suffer mightily from them. It's a big deal!

For instance, a female doctor once told me some women's body weights can fluctuate up to 30 pounds during their monthly cycles.

I cannot imagine how much even just five pounds means in a culture where women are judged first and foremost by their looks.

A husband who does not talk about it, sympathize, and try to help, should be replaced.

Your Friend Rick

Sergeant Sex

Letter 33

———— ✦ ————

Dear Robin,

In previous letters, I pointed out how important it is for both partners to be always aware our minds are programmed for the economy of the 20th and 21st centuries. But our bodies and brains are hard-wired for the economy of the Paleolithic.

When your loved one says or does something unseemly, it might be a good idea to ask yourself, did this come from his or her mind, or from the hard-wiring in his or her Stone Age brain?

When I was a teen, Robin, I lived in hormone hell. In matters of romance, this completely destroyed my judgment.

Unless they have some kind of physical abnormality, all males go through it. In the contest for dominance between love and sex, sex usually wins hands down.

Sex is like a drill sergeant. It grabs young males by the shirt collar, throws them up against a wall, and growls, "I'm in charge, Private Love, and don't ever forget it!"

Private Love whimpers, "Yes, sergeant, you bet sergeant, always, always sergeant."

In other words, in younger males, biochemistry is always trying to dominate affection.

In a healthy guy, Sergeant Sex does not begin to retire and back off until he is around age sixty or later. Only then can Private Love calmly begin to rule — to experience what his wife feels, or wants to feel, in the bedroom.

However, by then, I'm afraid, in many cases when a woman sees romance in a man's eye, she feels like a rabbit trying to sell a coyote on the virtues of vegetarianism.

It would be interesting to know how many times in her life the average woman says to herself, "Oh no, here he comes again," as her libido freezes solid.

I once heard another psychologist say, "A great many marriage difficulties are, fundamentally, sex problems. He wants to and she doesn't."

I am convinced a lot of guys are like me when I was young. They don't even know they have a testosterone problem.

A wise friend once pointed out to me that what makes a real man is a guy who can control his testosterone, and what makes a moron is a guy who is controlled by it.

But if you love him, you can help him. As I said in an earlier letter, I have tried to pack as much male experience and emotions into these letters as possible on the assumption at least some female readers truly want to know what makes their men tick and to help them.

But I'm afraid few women do. They have been victimized by uncivilized men so often that they have no sympathy for *any* man, even the ones they love, or ones who are doing their best to control their demons.

I am sure this is why few men reveal their demons. Most have learned that some women are too wounded or just plain delicate to handle these revelations, much less sympathize about them.

But some women aren't so delicate, and Samantha was one of them. I was astoundingly lucky to have ever met her, much less married her.

All that said, Robin, I am going to stick my neck out and suggest treating your lover's testosterone poisoning as a routine hygiene problem.

Emphasis on routine. Occasionally take a friendship shower. Her tiger killer steps in, and she follows with her bar of soap, with which, if needed, she is delightfully adept.

Under this continuing treatment of the problem, Sergeant Sex is demoted to private, and Private Love gets promoted to lieutenant.

You might do a search for "Which bath soap is gentlest on skin?"

Your Friend Rick

P.S. Of course, friendship showers may not work for you. Ladies, if you can come up with something that does a better job of defusing the testosterone bomb, more power to you! I am sure your husband will be forever grateful. He *needs* your help!

I wish every woman could spend one week with the biochemistry of a man. And vice versa, of course.

Excuses for Male Craziness

Letter 34

————— ◆ —————

Dear Robin,

I am sure some women will say I am just making excuses for male craziness. I'm giving guys a pass for being uncivilized.

But in my opinion, rare is the woman who can empathize with a man. To my mind, a man who never behaves like a crazed wild animal — a man who is *always* a gentleman — is heroic.

Unless he has a shortage of testosterone. Then I imagine his life can be much easier.

I kid you not. If he carries a normal load of that awful substance, or heaven forbid an excessive load, I am convinced it is mighty difficult for him to be happy, or even just content.

In fact, I suspect that, except as a formal dictionary definition, many men even know what the word contentment means. As adults, they have never experienced it except in the few minutes of afterglow.

I will forever be thankful to Samantha for understanding.

Your Friend Rick

P.S. I believe so many women have been so seriously mistreated as sex toys that they do not *want* to see things from a man's point of view.

I can't blame them. I'd probably feel the same way.

All I can say is that some guys do try to be gentlemen, and some even succeed. You might ask yours if he would read these letters and talk them over with you. Ask if he'd like help.

If he says yes, a possible place to start is for him to spend more time with other men who are trying to be gentlemen and less with those who are not.

I normally have little good to say about peer pressure, but sometimes it can help.

Hormones, They Aren't All Bad

Letter 35

———— ✦ ————

D ear Robin,

I am glad our recent correspondence caused you to ask about BHRT.

Samantha and I used Bioidentical Hormone Replacement Therapy for about 25 years. We have always been thankful to Dr. Johnathan Wright of the Tahoma Clinic near Seattle for getting us started on it. Dr. Wright is a pioneer in the field.

BHRT is not the same thing as HRT, Hormone Replacement Therapy.

HRT can use drugs that, although approved by the federal bureaucracy, are not your body's standard equipment. They are synthetic. For instance, Premarin® is made from horse urine.

BHRT uses the real stuff, hormones identical to those produced by the human body.

As far as we know, Sam and I never had any ill effects from the bioidentical variety, and the helpful effects have been great.

We have often been complimented on looking younger than our age. And, we have simply felt better — stronger, more lively, engaged, and mentally competent than other baby boomers.

BHRT greatly reduced Samantha's menopause symptoms, and not surprisingly, helped her feel more amorous.

In my non-medical layman's opinion, anyone over 40 owes it to themselves to talk with two or three compounding pharmacists and ask for their recommendations for MDs who do BHRT.

As with all medications, the usual precaution: work with a doctor and know possible side effects to watch for.

In many cases, I am sure, BHRT can be the single best thing a couple can do for their marriage.

Your Friend Rick

Pornography &
Testosterone Poisoning

Letter 36

————— ✦ —————

D ear Robin,

    I am reasonably certain that to enjoy a healthy bedroom relationship, a woman needs to feel good about herself.

I cannot imagine anything that would demolish her self-esteem faster than catching her husband viewing porn.

No surprise there. Humans are comparison shoppers.

I've been told by guys who have had numerous bed partners that after they married they wished they hadn't. When they are in bed with the women they hope to love for the rest of their lives, they think about the others.

Now take that difficulty and combine it with the flood of porn online.

A medical person who studies this problem has told me porn devastates marriages.

Worse, girls attending the mass-production, peer-pressure-cooker schools are already wired like violins trying to compete with other women — movie stars, models, homecoming queens, entertainers, the girl next door, you name it. To my mind, this is undoubtedly why the female teen suicide rate has soared. Robin, how many women can compete with perfection?

I once asked a gray-haired doctor, "In your experience, how many women really look like centerfolds?" He thought a moment and said, "Maybe one in a hundred."

So, using his estimate, one percent of wives are equipped to compare favorably to what their husbands' testosterone is searching for.

To that awful situation, add online dating. Robin, a marriage counselor told me a lot of adult guys are like kids in a toy store, flipping from one shiny new thing to another.

And, she said, this leads to ghosting — establishing a relationship just to sample the sex, then suddenly cutting it off with no warning and moving on to the next tantalizing package.

Robin, I cannot prove it, but I suspect that in the absence of an old-fashioned love affair, a marriage has practically no chance of success. So the number of people who should not get married is growing by leaps and bounds.

Again, humans are comparison shoppers. In my opinion, if you want a strong, lasting marriage, fight like a lion against the temptation to compare.

Your Friend Rick

P.S. Robin, marriage is something special. When done well, it is wonderful, fantastic, and spectacular. But it isn't easy. It's not something you just fall into. We could be wrong, but Samantha and I see marriage as a skill that must be learned, and continually honed and polished.

More About the Distance Between Women & Men

Letter 37

———— ✦ ————

Dear Robin,

At work, Samantha had a friend I will call Betty who was worried about her son. He was doing poorly in school because he would not concentrate on his studies.

In an anguished voice, Betty asked Sam, "What's wrong with his mind? Why can't he focus? There must be something wrong with him; *what's he thinking about?*"

The two women mulled it over, and then Sam came home and told me about Betty's problem.

I asked, "How old is he?"

"Fifteen."

"I can tell her what he's thinking about."

"Oh?"

"Of course. Breasts."

"Breasts!?"

The next day Sam passed this on to Betty, who exclaimed loudly, "Breasts!?"

When I tell this story people laugh. But believe me, if you are the young tiger killer, it's not so funny. No guy likes being obsessed with women's bodies. It gives women a power over us that no one should have.

I have heard a great many men complain about being slaves to women's magnetism. They experienced too many cases in which women flirted — teased them — then instead of delivering the goods, walked away with a haughty expression that silently boasted, "Look and weep, you will never touch this body."

Robin, I am not blaming all women for the behavior of stupid males. I am saying, if you don't want to get burned, don't play with matches, because the day may come when your luck will run out.

I can tell you for a fact that there are some men you absolutely do not want to tease, and *you have no way of knowing who they are.* I remember a male movie character — I don't remember who — saying to a female character, "Lady, you take a lot of chances."

Your Friend Rick

Understanding Even More About Testosterone

Letter 38

———— ✦ ————

D ear Robin,

In case you would like a bit deeper understanding of the testosterone-laden behavior of the typical young male, let me tell you a brief story.

I once watched an interview of an older man who had been a fighter pilot in the skies over Germany in WWII.

Robin, please understand that aerial combat involves being shot at by heavy machine guns, and light canons with explosive warheads.

This, while the pilot sits atop a fuel tank containing hundreds of gallons of high-octane gasoline.

The former pilot explained this to the interviewer, who was horrified and exclaimed something like, "It must have been awful!"

With a grin and a rise in his voice, the pilot exclaimed, "Awful?"

"Are you kidding? I WAS TWENTY YEARS OLD AND I WAS FLYING A P-51!"

Your Friend Rick

Shyness

Letter 39

———— ✦ ————

Dear Robin,

As a young person, I was so hormonal that as I walked along the high school and college hallways you could hear the testosterone sloshing in my tennis shoes.

No one ever said a word to me about my biochemistry. No one took me aside one day and warned, "Get used to it kid, you will be living in hormone hell for the next fifty years. The only time you will be fully rational is when you're asleep."

As I see it, shyness is nature's way of keeping young men and women apart until they are ready for the responsibilities of being together.

But schools, which are mass-production, peer-pressure-cookers, see shyness as bad. School culture uses dances, sports, clubs, and other social activities to break down shyness as early as possible. They even use popularity as a factor in judging a young person's success in school.

I think this deliberate destruction of shyness works so well it is a major contributor to the epidemic of teen sex, teen pregnancy, and teen abortion.

Your Friend Rick

"In the first place, God made idiots. This was for practice. Then He made school boards." — Mark Twain

P.S. A reminder: this book is actually two books, and I promise you will love Book Two, the *Owner's Manual*. It's the real prize.

Beware of John Wayne

Letter 40

Dear Robin,

For young males, this letter might be obsolete. I hope so.

But for middle-aged and older males, including my generation, I think it is crucially important, not only for the guys but women, too.

Born in 1907, John Wayne, "The Duke," was a movie actor who may have been the most popular ever. Starring in 142 motion pictures — usually westerns and war films — he became the icon of American manhood.

When I was young, every guy felt pressure to be what Wayne portrayed in his most famous roles. He was strong, tall, handsome, courageous, individualistic, patriotic, protective and nearly bullet-proof.

One of his best friends, director and producer John Ford, helped teach him how to portray this hyper-masculinity.

I remember another friend of Wayne's being interviewed. She said, "Nobody is John Wayne, not even John Wayne."

But that's who males saw on the screen, and in all too many cases judged themselves against.

I remember in the Vietnam War, a buddy of mine who was a Marine said that in boot camp, the trainees were sent to the movie theater to watch Wayne's World War II movie, *Sands of Iwo Jima,* week after week, over and over.

How much of Wayne is still left in American culture, I don't know. But I advise each woman to watch some of his movies so they can spot Wayneism if it pops up in their lives, especially in their marriages.

This is not to say Wayneism is all bad. The day could come in a man's life when he really does need to perform like a Wayne character, to protect others. I am all for that, and in fact had to do it once. But his wife should assure him he does not need to be John Wayne all day every day.

By the way, speaking from been-there-and-done-that experience to any guys reading this, if you ever need to do it, you will. You won't chicken out. You will *automatically* throw yourself into the challenge.

But training helps a lot, and I recommend it. Learn the techniques of firefighting, water rescue, first aid, shooting, and anything else that might be needed to save a loved one. Be good at it and stay good.

One of Wayne's most persuasive movies is *They Were Expendable.* I watch it every five years or so to remind me of how subtle and persuasive war propaganda can be.

I challenge any heterosexual male to watch it all the way through without feeling an intense urge to run down to the nearest recruiter and sign up.

If I were the father of a son in his teens, twenties, or thirties, I'd ask him to watch the movie with me and notice his own emotions throughout, especially at the end. Then discuss exactly how the movie evokes these almost irresistible feelings.

Your Friend Rick

That Awful Three-Letter Word

Letter 41

———— ◆ ————

D ear Robin,

Sex. I get the impression many men are comfortable with the word and use it freely. They even use its harsh four-letter synonym freely when referring to closeness with the women they love. I think many see sex as something they do *to* women, not *with* women.

As a writer, meaning a professional wordsmith, I pay attention to the nuances of words. In addition to their dictionary meanings, many words have subtleties, tones, and distinctions.

Robin, sex is one of them. One syllable. Only three letters.

This gives the word an inherent feeling of get-it-over-with-fast.

I doubt this is something a woman in deep, lasting love wants to hear.

Compare it to the word intimacy. Four syllables, eight letters.

Intimacy implies emotion, gentleness, caring, patience, contentment, fulfillment.

What sounds more appealing, a quick jab, or a slow caress?

Perhaps the most helpful practice in all relationships of every kind is, keep an open mind; **always try to see things from the other person's point of view!**

By the way, today a common school of thought is that sex is just a normal bodily function. All animals do it, and humans are animals. Don't obsess over it. Just enjoy it. If you aren't bed-hopping, you must have hang-ups.

Do you really believe what happens in a bedroom is no different than what goes on in a chicken coop?

That view is a product of the "sexual revolution," which should be called the sexual catastrophe, as I will write about in my next letter.

Your Friend Rick

More About That Awful Word

Letter 42

————— ♦ —————

Dear Robin,

I greatly dislike using that three-letter word, but for my topic today, nothing is more appropriate.

Here is my main point: no one knows much about sex.

All anyone understands with any certainty is the biological part. Tab A fits into slot B, then there are a few moments of hopefully pleasurable sensation, followed by some mind-boggling microbiology.

The microbiology may be the only facet of sex backed by cold, hard science instead of opinion.

You can read a thousand books about it, but controlled double-blind scientific experiments about sex are few and far between.

In Samantha's and my thinking, the few moments of bodily connection are about five percent of the story, and the other ninety-five are all mystery.

Why? Because, no one knows much about the psychological, emotional, or spiritual facets of sex. Robin, there are lots of opinions, but how much scientific evidence?

Yet kids in school are taught "sex education," which leads them to think that after they have absorbed this "education," they know what they are doing.

I have bad news for them. When it comes to sex, no one knows what they are doing.

Here is an example. What percentage of your bedroom intimacy is love, and what percentage is lust?

If you can't measure it, it's not science, it's guesswork. And about sex, it certainly varies from person to person, and day to day.

So who could know much about it?

Too many sex-ed courses begin with the assumption there is someone who does. But no one does, and no one can. Again, we are all different and changing endlessly. How long could any findings be good for?

I repeat, I am not talking about the biology or mechanics of sex. Those are well understood. But in my opinion, they are only 5% of the story. The other 95% is the emotions, psychology, and especially the spirituality.

What percentage of what we experience in bed is spiritual? No one knows. I think it probably varies from person to person, and day to day.

I can't look inside someone's soul and understand what is going on there. Indeed, it's a mighty challenge to look inside my own soul. That's where the term soul-searching comes from.

Here is what I call a *Big Truth* that's been buried for at least a half-century. Possibly the most enjoyable, or even thrilling part of marriage is from *exploring* that mystery — exploring the unknown 95% — together.

But that's an old-fashioned view. I'm guessing modern thinkers will say there are no provable spiritual, emotional, or psychological aspects to sex — it's all just biological in one way or another — same as what happens in that chicken coop.

If you do not have a spirit, you can skip the rest of this book.

But if you do have one, I suggest you invite it to participate in the bedroom activities.

Samantha and I were married 56 years and studied scores of books about marriage. But when it came to the bedroom, we still had a lot more questions than answers.

Next letter, more about that all-consuming mystery.

Your Friend Rick

"Love seems the swiftest, but it is the slowest of all growths. No man or woman really knows what perfect love is until they have been married a quarter century." — Mark Twain

The Fatal Attraction, & More About How Much We Don't Know

Letter 43

————— ♦ —————

Dear Robin,

I recently read an interview of a sex ed teacher who kept referring to "body systems." This guy, apparently a modern thinker, believes sex is about bodies, when in fact, in Samantha's and my estimation, 95% is in the head and heart.

As I said in an earlier letter, to us the biggest mystery is the spiritual one. Wow! It *really* is mind-boggling. But I wonder how many people have ever considered that there even *is* a spiritual facet to bedroom activities.

What, you thought it was possible to weld two bodies together without also welding their spirits?

Robin, have you ever wondered how long the weld lasts, or if there is damage when it is broken?

Or even if, when in bed, we have a *choice* to weld spiritually or not.

Let me emphasize that. In the bedroom, can we decide *not* to have emotional, psychological, or spiritual bonding?

If I were raising a child these days, when it came to "the talk," I'd lay heavy emphasis on the fact that most of sex remains uncharted territory.

To Samantha and me, judging by the experiences of friends, sex without commitment is playing with dynamite.

Especially for the woman.

I suspect her Stone Age DNA is programmed to bond. Like it or not, she is hard-wired to find a man, a protector, before her later months of pregnancy and helplessness arrive.

In the 21st century, she isn't helpless, of course, but nature wired her for the Paleolithic.

I remember a close friend of Sam's. The young woman would sometimes get "the itch," and go to bed with almost any guy, including ones she wouldn't trust to wash her car.

She'd have an understanding with them: this is just for fun, no promises. The next day she'd be madly in love with the jerk and would begin following him around like a puppy.

Again, our minds are from the 20th and 21st centuries, but our bodies and brains are from the Stone Age.

Here is my guess about what is happening.

In the final two months of pregnancy, a Stone Age woman was helpless. She couldn't run and couldn't fight. When the sabertooth tiger came near, she needed a strong, tough man to protect her and her children.

The women who survived to carry on the species were likely ones who would sleep with a guy, and then latch on to him like a barnacle.

It is known that in the bedroom a woman's hypothalamus and pituitary gland automatically produce oxytocin, which is called "the love hormone."

Let me emphasize, Robin, production of such substances is automatic, she cannot control it.

This sexual biochemistry might also explain the common phenomenon of the woman who is drawn to "bad boys."

I think her "Paleolithic DNA"[1] not only wants a protector, it wants one that is ferocious — a warrior — and she will stay attached to him no matter how badly he treats her. In the Paleolithic, the lives of her children depended on it.

I'm sure I have heard the male side of this barnacle story dozens of times. "I was totally honest! I told her over and over, this is just for fun! No commitments! And now everywhere I go, there she is!"

Yes, like the 1987 movie *Fatal Attraction*.

Being old-fashioned to the core, I think the sexual revolution is the worst thing that ever happened to women. Surely, bedroom intimacy without commitment has turned them into sex toys like nothing ever seen before.

And, I'm convinced pornography has greatly magnified this. Too often now, I think, women are not just courted, they are hunted.

Again, everyone knows about sex, but except for the cold, hard biology, no one *understands* much about it.

The emotional, psychological and especially spiritual sides remain monumental unknowns. If there are young people in your life, I hope you will warn them.

If I go down in history for just one paragraph of my writing, I hope it is that one.

Again, in my estimation, of what there is to know about the subject of sex, only about five percent is understood. And I think women know this intuitively. But these days they are taught to ignore it.

Men? I think most are blinded by their testosterone. Until they fall deeply and undeniably in love, I suspect these days most — but not all — are just looking for momentary relief. They will say or do whatever it takes to satisfy their Stone Age drive.

But you already knew that, didn't you, Robin?

There is great truth in the old locker room comment, why buy a cow when you can get the milk for free?

A final point. Exploring the bedroom mysteries within the security of marriage can be really, really fun because the *automatic bonding* is a colossal fringe benefit instead of a monumental disaster.

Your Friend Rick

P.S. Well, maybe not the final point. It was not till age 69, when my testosterone load plunged and my equipment finally broke down completely, that I began to realize how much, for so many years, sex had gotten in the way of love.

Once the testosterone began to diminish, love was more free
to come to the surface. And it has stayed there.

Truly, at 69 I finally understood how much the
forced obsession with women's bodies had distracted
and dominated me throughout my teens and adulthood.
Suddenly I felt as if I'd been let out of prison.

I am so wonderfully grateful to Samantha for being so
understanding and helpful during our earlier years.

My love for her was, and still is, more fierce than anything
my libido ever cooked up.

My God, how I love that woman, more every day.

**"People talk about beautiful friendships
between two persons of the same sex.
What is the best of that sort, as compared
with the friendship of man and wife,
where the best impulses and highest ideals
of both are the same? There no place for
comparison between the two friendships;
the one is earthly, the other divine."
— Mark Twain**

---

1. This expression is my invention, not a standard scientific term.

Touching

Letter 44

————— ◆ —————

Dear Robin,

Touching. I enjoyed it a lot, and Samantha yearned for it.

Passing each other in the hallway, we'd brush.

Walking between our house and our offices, we'd hold hands.

Riding in the car, the passenger would keep a hand on the driver's leg.

Walking down the street, more hand-holding.

Watching TV on the sofa, one would lean back into the embrace of the other.

At lunch in a restaurant, we'd hold hands across the table while diving into long, fascinating conversations about every imaginable topic.

By the way, Robin, I strongly suggest you give restaurant hand-holding a try. You might be surprised at how it can improve the service if the server is female.

As I mentioned earlier, when touching a loved one, the body produces oxytocin, or "the love hormone" or "bonding hormone." The more you cuddle, hold hands, walk arm in arm, kiss, and caress, the closer you grow emotionally.

The thing Samantha and I are most grateful for in our 56-year honeymoon is we touched every chance we got. Neither of us has ever experienced anything more pleasurable than skin against skin.

When I remember it, I tear up.

Even when walking between our house and the swimming pool (18 paces), or the house and our offices (44 paces), we'd hold hands.

Touching also had an important practical application. When a series of customary touches did not happen, this was a silent signal that, maybe there is something we need to talk about.

Touching in public was common when Samantha and I were young. In high school and college, the hallways were often blocked by couples walking hand-in-hand.

Today we see hand-holding only rarely. We don't know why, but we are sure the world is poorer without it. (It may be a regional phenomenon, happening in some places but not in others.)

One day, after I had begun writing these letters, I spent an hour at a crowded art fair in the park. Among at least a thousand people, I counted four couples touching. Three of these appeared as old or older than Samantha and me, and only one couple was young.

Maybe old-fashioned love is the only kind that's left.

It's become so uncommon that one day as Sam and I were holding hands while walking into a building, a woman coming out, stopped us and inquired, "I'm sorry, is someone ill?"

Summarizing, to Samantha and me, there is just no such thing as too much touching. Indeed, it may not be an exaggeration to say if the touching never stops, the courting never stops.

By the way, Robin, if you have children, I am confident they will not be harmed by observing lifelong affection.

Your Friend Rick

P.S. There is also this possibility. The more touching, the more comfortable the lady will feel about being touched. She will no longer fear that every contact must lead to the bedroom.

Women Are Not Sex Toys

Letter 45

———— ✦ ————

D ear Robin,

Back to the Paleolithic. As I said earlier, a woman is designed to have babies. In the Stone Age, pregnancy made her virtually helpless for months. She could not run and could not fight.

To fend off the sabertooth tigers, she needed a man for more than one night.

When I was in college during the 1960s, the "sexual revolution" was sweeping through high schools and colleges. It was most visible at the famous 1969 Woodstock orgy.

The sexual revolution also brought with it the "A-for-a-lay" practice. High school and college women would trade their bodies for higher grades.

Whether this is still common, and used by female instructors, too, I don't know.

Assuming what young people have told me is true, many women now see sex through male eyes. It's just a biological urge like breathing, eating, drinking, and sleeping. Nothing emotional, psychological, or spiritual to it.

I'm guessing this attitude originated from male college instructors equipped with glib arguments about a coed's need to do what comes naturally.

One result, in my opinion, is that women today are sex toys like none ever seen before.

I say to guys, stay aware that, in my opinion, she probably has some emotional damage from being treated like an object, a thing — a receptacle — who was often deceived about a man's real intentions.

Your Friend Rick

P.S. I have said to women, if I were a single lady my standard procedure on the first date would be to warn the guy, no sex till the honeymoon.

The women usually answer, then you will never have any second dates.

Sometimes when I think of the cruelty inflicted on women, both emotional and physical, just because they want to be loved, I first feel a deep sadness, and then rage.

Commitment

Letter 46

─────────── ◆ ───────────

Dear Robin,

I have long believed the ancient rule of no sex outside marriage contained much wisdom. It was an excellent test of whether or not a man had the willpower, the tenacity, to be marriage material.

For instance, if he could not follow that rule, then what would happen when the going got tough?

Would the husband hang in there with his mate, especially if there were children?

Suppose, for example, a family is hit by what millions have in the past. They have children, a mortgage, and car payments, then the Federal Reserve tightens the money supply.

Both lose their jobs, then their home, then their cars. They suddenly find themselves living on the street.

What is a prospective husband made of? When the family's life crashes — and it easily can these days, the Federal Reserve is not going out of business — will the husband hang in there with his wife and their children, or cut and run?

If he has never been tested long-term on something difficult, how can a woman know?

Let me point out, however, that if children are not in the cards, it may not be all that important. These days, in many cases I have seen, a woman living alone and supporting herself is better off than she would be living with a man.

Your Friend Rick

Where Our Happiness Came From

Letter 47

———— ◆ ————

D ear Robin,

Marital happiness was easy for Samantha and me to come by. Without fail, the best way to make myself happy was to do things that made Samantha happy, and vice versa.

I was, for instance, always inventing things to make her life better. When the government's draft dragged me into the Air Force, I was paid starvation wages. Using its Consumer Price Index Calculator, in today's money, I was getting $849 dollars per month.

So, Sam and I lived in a slum. The apartment had no shower curtain, so I made one out of a parachute. She was delighted.

There was a kitchen sink, but no counter. Using coat hangers and boards, I improvised one.

The gear shift on our Volkswagen bug had a long, loose throw that was slow and difficult for her. I installed a device called a Slick Shifter, which shortened and quickened it.

Later, in every house we ever owned, I built her a separate workbench for her hobbies and projects.

In return, over the years, she sewed patches in my clothing, baked me heavenly chocolate chip cookies, gave me lessons in how to operate the TV, and invented really, really fantastic kisses.

In short, doing for each other caused bonding. More about this, Robin, in my next letter.

Your Friend Rick

The Importance of Nurturing

Letter 48

———— ✦ ————

D ear Robin,
   One of my biggest mistakes, and biggest shocks, had to do with nurturing.

I have always strived to be independent, a textbook "American rugged individualist." To me, if someone did something for me, then I owed them, and I deplore being in debt. To me, debt is slavery.

For the first 33 years of our marriage, I strived mightily to never be any kind of burden on Sam (or, for that matter, anyone else.) I loathed the thought of being a nuisance, and did not want to be taken care of even when I was sick.

One day I was talking with my counselor, and mentioned this.

Robin, she was shocked. She asked, "But what if Samantha *wants* to take care of you?"

The possibility had never crossed my mind.

The counselor proceeded to lecture me for being cruel to my wife.

She explained that some people, especially women, want to nurture those they care about. The nurturing impulse or instinct can be quite strong — part and parcel of loving someone.

This was all news to me.

Samantha dearest, my heartfelt apologies.

I immediately took the counselor's advice to heart, and from then on welcomed Samantha's nurturing, and was surprised and pleased to find her enjoying it. So I enjoyed it, too.

Your Friend Rick

P.S. Nurturing should not be limited to physical matters. A person's emotions and self-esteem are equally important. We often complimented each other about our looks, accomplishments, or skills. The key to this is sincerity. The remark must be honest. *Never stop courting your loved one!*

"I can live for two months on a good compliment." — Mark Twain

I'm Coming!

Letter 49

———— ✦ ————

Dear Robin,

If I remember correctly, in one part of the 1986 movie *Top Gun*, Tom Cruise is a fighter pilot, flying hell-bent for leather to the rescue of his buddy who is losing a vicious air battle. Cruise is yelling into the radio "I'M COMING! I'M COMING!"

I would tell any single woman, if you are looking for a husband, that's the kind you should be searching for. If you are in trouble, he will move heaven and earth to get to you.

I try to have people like that in my life. If I am in trouble, they absolutely, positively *will* show up. And, of course, I try to be that kind of friend to them.

It was a fundamental part of Sam's and my marriage. If one of us was in jeopardy, we knew the other would be there, no matter what.

But knowing was not enough. We would occasionally remind each other of it.

I am writing here again not about what is 21st century logical, but what is in our Stone Age DNA. We want to *hear and feel* the security, even if we do not actually need it.

If you have a spouse — or with close friends — remind them occasionally, "If you are in trouble, I will be there, no matter what. I *will* find a way to get to you."

Guys, she is designed to have children, and whether she actually does or not, her number one priority is to *know* her man is always ready to risk life and limb to come to her rescue.

Guys, try this occasionally. In a loud, strong voice say to her, "If you need me, I will *always* find a way to get to you!"

When I did that for Samantha, she replied that she too would always find a way to get to me.

Your Friend Rick

P.S. Another of our favorite songs is "How to Handle a Woman," from the movie and Broadway musical *Camelot*. Now *that's* a real love song, I hope you will give it a try.

Valentine's Day

Letter 50

————— ◆ —————

D ear Robin,
Samantha's favorite holiday was Christmas. All year long she would create hand-made Christmas ornaments.

My favorite holiday was Valentine's Day, because it was about our feelings for each other. Here is a letter she wrote me on our last Valentine's Day, a few months before she suddenly passed with no warning.

Your Friend Rick

My Dearest Husband, February 14, 2023
HAPPY ST. VALENTINE'S DAY!
If someone asked me what the most important day in my life has been, I would immediately reply, the day we met in November 1964!

When I think about the adventure we have had so far, there are so many wonderful memories, challenges we adapted to, and the love we still have for each other today.

I don't know why people see us as a different couple, but I am glad they do — because we are.

We travel our own road, not the one most people choose. We make our decisions together and move forward. We have an amazing marriage and I wouldn't trade it for anything in the world.

I will always love you with everything I am and from the bottom of my heart. You are such a special man, my husband, best friend, lover, business partner, and soul mate.

Here's to celebrating another 58 Valentine's Days together!!

All my love,

Sam

Notes

Book One – Part 4

Dealing with Others Outside the Marriage

In the Doctor's Office

Letter 51

———— ✦ ————

Dear Robin,

You asked how Sam and I managed our medical care.

We always went to our doctors together. Here's the story.

These days a doctor is so swamped by government bureaucracy, red tape, and general confusion that there's little time left for the patient. Things are hurried, and it can take two non-medical people to absorb the information a medical person is trying to deliver in too little time.

We'd long had a habit, which served us well as the quality of our medical care deteriorated.

In the exam room, Robin, one of us took notes while the other did question-and-answer with the doctor or the assistant. We'd also continually swap roles. I would be crafting a question while Sam was talking with the doctor, then while I was asking my question, Sam would be devising her next one.

By the end of the too-brief appointment, the doctor was exhausted from the back-and-forth grilling — it reminds me of a tennis match — but we got the information we needed.

Visiting our doctors together was also a safety precaution. Several years ago Samantha had a sudden spike in her blood pressure, to the point that her thinking was degraded.

I rushed her to the emergency room. The admitting nurse put her in a wheelchair, then began working with the computer. I stayed riveted to Sam.

As the woman pounded away at the keyboard, going from page to page meticulously entering whatever the government's programs ordered her to, Samantha grew worse.

I realized Sam's brain was shutting down.

I said, "She's altered."

The nurse stayed glued to the computer.

I said again loudly, "She's altered. Do something."

No response. Still glued to the screen.

This happened once or twice more, with the nurse still completely absorbed with the government's programming, not the patient.

Finally, my inner tiger killer woke up and I thought, I haven't given military orders in more than forty years, I wonder if I can still do it.

I jumped up and at the top of my voice began hollering, "Do something! Do something! Now! Now! Do something! Now! Now! *Doooooo something!!!*"

I was in the nurse's face, blasting away, like a drill sergeant. Little by little she tore her eyes from the screen and slowly turned toward me.

Robin, doors up and down the hallway banged open and perhaps a dozen other medical people came running to Sam's rescue.

If I had not been by her side ready to protect her, she would have died. Later, three times, that nurse came up to me greatly embarrassed, and apologized profusely.

Lesson: these days, under the runaway red tape, bureaucracy, and general confusion of the government-controlled medical system, if you are by yourself in a medical facility, you are alone.

Another benefit of always seeing a doctor together was, we were well-informed about each other's conditions and problems, so we were better at spotting each other's signs and symptoms early.

My advice Robin: you are not each other's property, but you are a team. Have the attitude that it's the two of you and the medical pros against the political madness.

Your Friend Rick

Be Always Ready for Tough Choices

Letter 52

———— ◆ ————

Dear Robin,

Almost from the day Samantha and I met, her parents did not like me.

When we got engaged they went ballistic.

It's understandable. At age 20, I was no prize. I had not yet learned how to control the testosterone.

In fact, I didn't even know men had testosterone or any other hormones; no one ever told me.

After the wedding, her parents went on a campaign to get us divorced, using a wide variety of underhanded ploys to destroy Samantha's trust in me.

It nearly worked, often causing us great pain and sorrow, not to mention many nights of me sleeping on the sofa.

One of her mother's ploys was to subtly, over and over, weave into conversations with Samantha, "All men cheat."

How would you defend yourself against that charge?

But my dear wife was smart and made of mighty tough stuff. She figured out what they were doing. Then one day she simply walked out of their house and never talked with them again. It was the last they ever saw or heard from her for the rest of their lives.

They had forced her to make a choice, so she did.

Another example. A young woman I once knew was a drama queen and an unrestrained flirt. She trifled unmercifully with numerous young men, playing damsel in distress.

Robin, she even went after a young priest.

The priest finally took the bait and tried to kiss her.

She spread the word: "Did you hear what father so-and-so did to me? Well, let me tell you!"

I do not know everything that happened after that, but I can imagine what happened to the priest's reputation, and possibly his career.

Her father wanted to throw the flirt out of the house, but the mother was loyal to her child. She said to the father, "If you throw her out, I'm throwing you out."

It was a Hobson's choice.[1]

The father backed down, and their marriage was never again the same.

Sometimes life is hard.

I could be wrong, but it seems to me that in the final analysis, men are about women, and women are about children. In the Hobson's choice between the husband and the kids, the guy comes in second.

I think it's in the DNA. Guys are expendable and kids are not.

When I originally wrote this letter I said, "I cannot overemphasize the importance of putting your spouse and your marriage first ahead of everybody."

A mother set me straight. In most cases involving the kids, it's not going to happen.

The kernel of the problem is that humans, including offspring, have free wills, and sometimes they make bad choices that force the parents to go down the Hobson Road.

If you have children or plan to have them, all I can suggest is that you talk this over before a child forces you to confront it.

My next letter might help.

Your Friend Rick

---

1. Hobson's choice. A choice between two equally awful alternatives.

Children

Letter 53

———— • ————

D ear Robin,

Thanks for your letter requesting more about children.

Samantha and I are not the people to ask. We did not have any.

Granted, we were both teachers, me for four years and Samantha for eight. But that's not the same thing as being parents.

But I can promise you this. Once you have been through the *Owner's Manual*, you will have your marriage running so smoothly that making those large life-changing decisions and day-to-day small ones about children, or anything else, will be far easier and more likely to be successful.

Your Friend Rick

P.S. Some may wonder why Samantha and I did not have children.

She suffered such horrific physical and emotional abuse in childhood that when the subject would come up, she'd say to me, "I'm afraid I would raise my kids the way I was raised."

It was no idle concern. As early as 1987, a Federal Department of Justice survey of the literature[1] found that "about one-third of all individuals who were physically abused, sexually abused, or extremely neglected will subject their children to one of these forms of maltreatment."

Also, "the rate of abuse among individuals with a history of abuse is approximately six times higher than the base rate for abuse in the general population."

Sam loved kids so much she refused to take the risk.

---

1. "Do Abused Children Become Abusive Parents?" *Department of Justice* website, Office of Justice Programs, 1987.

Ethics vs. Loyalty

Letter 54

———— ♦ ————

Dear Robin,

As I said in my last letter, I originally wrote that the marriage must come first ahead of "everybody."

I did not say ahead of ethics.

It *will* happen, count on it. There will be a family member, friend, or someone else important in your life who will tolerate somebody's unethical behavior.

The two will expect you to side with them.

Do not fall for it. If an unethical person expects you to remain loyal to them, then you will be painted with the same brush they are.

In my opinion, every married couple should talk over the clash between ethics and loyalty. They should decide ahead of time which they will choose together *as a couple* if ever they are forced to — because in a marriage, one spouse's reputation is the other spouse's reputation.

As for a mother's dedication to her child, I like to think that if Samantha and I had run into the Hobson's choice problem, we would have decided ahead of time that we'd go with what is ethical.

Much more about ethics and choices in the *Owner's Manual*. It's critically important, and I think it will solve any Hobson's choice problems you might run into.

By the way, in regard to reputations, one of the wisest and most lucrative things ever said to me when I was young came from an older friend named Blair Painter. Blair advised me to "always behave as if you are applying for a job, because you are."

Today I would add, and you are applying for jobs for your spouse, too.

If you are not married yet but are contemplating it, you might ask yourself, do I want this person's reputation?

Your Friend Rick

Attractiveness

Letter 55

———— ◆ ————

Dear Robin,

I suspect the old saying that beauty is in the eye of the beholder is far more true than most realize.

Contrary to what is pounded into adolescent heads by the mass-production, peer-pressure-cooker schools, there is no single standard of beauty.

I think the day will come when people will look back on what schools do to a person's mind and emotions, and be horrified.

Among other things, Robin, the boys memorize centerfolds, then comb through the female population looking for girls with those specifications. It's sick.

You probably know grown men who, even though they are over 60, are still looking for women with teenage dimensions.

My personal estimate is that few males get over this obsession with looks before their fifties, and I'm guessing few females ever do. I think in the US at age 60, many women still feel bad about not looking like the homecoming queen at 18.

In any case, my point again is, there are many kinds of beauty. A sunset, a Monet painting, a mathematical equation, a Boeing 777, a bottlenose dolphin. All are gorgeous.

I love Samantha's mind and emotions so much that whatever her physical appearance happened to be — and it changed many times over the years — it was lovely to me.

I can look at photos of her from decade after decade, and they all still appeal to me, regardless of her dimensions or skin condition at any given time. I love *her*, not her outward appearance.

Robin, believe it or not, even on Sam's departure day, when she was in the throes of the cancer, she had a special kind of loveliness I'd never seen before. It shook me, I will never forget it, and I cannot explain it.

(In other words, my dear wife, by being who you are, you carved out your own unique niche in the world of beauty. To me you are and always will be stunning.)

Your Friend Rick

P.S. By the way, Robin, here is an insight that might be useful to women. In my forties, as my maturity and judgment improved (yes, guys, it eventually does!) I began to notice I was seeing women less as sex objects and more as works of art. And, in writing this, I just realized this delightful trend continues to this day. Perhaps the observation will help some women style themselves to impress a better class of males.

And by the way, to me, Samantha was never a what, a trophy. She was a who. I wanted to get to know her better and better. Here, I think, is a key point. Undoubtedly the questions I asked her most often in our 56 years began with, "What do you think about...?"

Sam, thank you, you taught me so much.

The New Socialist Undefined Man

Letter 56

————— ◆ —————

Dear Robin,

In the beginning of his book *The New Socialist Man* (1969), Theodore Hsi-en Chen explains:

"A new society presupposes new men with new minds, new emotions, and new attitudes."

That is the premise of socialism. Humans can and should be altered into a new kind of creature, the New Socialist Man.

This flies in the face of what we know about humans. I find it rather entertaining that a premise of socialism is that our Paleolithic programming can be changed.

It can be adapted to, certainly, but not altered, at least not yet. It's in the DNA.

By the way, this socialist assumption that schooling can alter our genetic makeup — that it can make a person into the "new socialist man" — is where today's school industry came from.

In the early 20th century, education "reformers" such as John Dewey believed "Gary Plan" mass-production schooling, also known as "platoon schools," should be forced on all parents and children. And until the home education movement came along, it had been.

It's been forced onto the teachers, too. They are victims just as much as the kids and parents.

Your parents and probably teachers, too, were never told about this hidden school agenda, and this likely has a big effect on your marriage. Next letter.

Your Friend Rick

"I was educated once. It took me years to get over it." — Mark Twain

P.S. I hope you read the revealing eight-minute article, "How John Dewey Used Public 'Education' to Subvert Liberty," by Alex Newman, Illinois Family Institute website, March 13, 2021.

Know Your Enemy

Letter 57

———— ♦ ————

D ear Robin,

A main principle of socialism is that, no matter what the problem, the solution is more government.

Under the socialist movement, governments have grown so large and powerful that, whether we recognize it or not, they now encroach on nearly every aspect of our lives.

For example, Robin, wages we work for, prices we pay, interest rates we earn on our savings, what we will or won't be allowed to buy with our hard-earned money, the opinions our children will be required to memorize in school, and who will teach these opinions — all and more are directly or indirectly forced onto us by Congress, the Federal Reserve, the President and hundreds of other federal, state and local political agencies.

The federal government alone — not the state or local ones, just federal — has made up more than 300,000 laws,[1] and each American is held responsible for knowing and obeying those that apply to him or her.

Ignorance of the law is no excuse.

The 300,000 made-up laws force the American people to spend 9.8 billion manhours on paperwork each year.[2] Yes, that's a billion with a b.

Politicians even have us all changing our clocks in fall and spring. And they control the school industry, which means they control what teachers are forced to pour into the minds of the children. And some of those children grow up to be teachers.

Here is my point.

When I was young, politics was a trivial matter, mostly for friendly debate.

Now government is so deep into our pocketbooks, careers, businesses, and personal lives that it is commonly a cause of hard feelings and broken friendships, *including in some cases shattered families.*

In short, if you and your spouse do not share the same political opinions, politics can be bad for your marriage, because politics today intrudes on nearly every part of our lives.

To me, politics is a social disease.

In an article titled "Today's Politics Divide Parties, and Friends and Families, Too," a *New York Times* poll reports, "nearly one in five voters said that politics hurt their friendships or family relationships."[3]

The *Economist* magazine found that "More than three out of five Americans now say they avoid airing their political views for fear of suffering adverse consequences;

only a quarter of college students say they are comfortable discussing controversial topics with their peers."[4]

Samantha and I have known couples who became divided by their politics.

It's hardly avoidable.

Government invades so much of our lives now that it is a member of the family. And the most expensive one.

So, **know your enemy.** It is not your spouse, friends, or loved ones, **it's the government.**

As President Reagan warned over and over, "Government is not the solution, it's the problem."

Polling data from 20 countries, including the US, paint a grim picture for marriage.

Whereas two decades ago there was little difference between the number of women and men age 18-29 who leaned socialist, today women lean that way by a whopping margin of 25%.

This may be because so many more women than men now go to college, 46% vs. 35%,[5] where socialism is covertly injected into numerous courses, for the purpose of creating the new socialist man.

Robin, learn all you can about politics, economics, and related matters so that you and your spouse can work together to keep government from undermining your love for each other.

As a place to start, I hope you will try my Uncle Eric books. *Whatever Happened to Penny Candy?* which is very easy reading and takes only an hour to absorb, would be a good first taste.

Your Friend Rick

P.S. A close friend asks, "Can we be American and not be political?"

My answer is a very loud, "Yes," if you are trying to put America back on the path to the System of Liberty.

This system is nearly gone now, and what is left is almost completely misunderstood.

I doubt one in a hundred Americans any longer understands how the System of Liberty works, or even that there ever was such a system.

But reversing this sad decline is what my award-winning Uncle Eric books are designed to accomplish.

If you want to get political, I suggest you be guided by this motto: "Less government today, even less tomorrow, and so on, till you need a microscope to find it."

That is the motto of Samantha's and my company, Henry Madison Research, Inc.

To get started on the how-to of the return to the System of Liberty, I suggest you also look up the Reason Foundation, which was endorsed by British Prime Minister Margaret Thatcher.

1. "Many Failed Efforts to Count Nation's...," *Wall Street Journal* website, July 23, 2011; "Overcriminalization," *Heritage Foundation* website, 2023; "Three Felonies per day", by Harvey A. Silverglate, *Encounter Books*, 2009. "Go Directly to Jail — The Criminalization of Almost Everything", by Gene Healy, *Cato Institute*, 2004, p.21 & 24.

2. "The Laffer Curve of Law," interview with Supreme Court Justice Neil Gorsuch, *Wall Street Journal*, Aug 3-4, 2024, p.A11.

3. October 18, 2022.

4. III liberals, *The Economist*, Oct. 21, 2023, p.72.

5. "Young men and women are drifting apart," *The Economist*, March 16. 2024, p.12. The percentages are of degree holders.

Why Is Life So Hard

Letter 58

———— ◆ ————

D ear Robin,

Here's a shocker.

It's long been the case that one of the foremost causes of friction and arguing in a marriage is money. Now we know why.

Economists at MIT and Harvard have found that 90% of American children born in 1940 were eventually better off economically than their parents. But only around 50% born in the 1980s were, and the decline continues.[1]

Long ago I did individual in-home financial counseling. In almost every case where both parents worked outside the home, I found that when all hidden and unhidden taxes were taken into account, one spouse was supporting the family and the other was supporting the government.

In single-parent homes, the one parent was supporting both.

Now add this to the picture: The vast majority of the 1940 couples — the most successful ones — had only one person working outside the home.

And, note this: In those days the wife was seen as a backup, able to get a job if her husband became ill. Today these reserves are already in the battle, yet we're still going backwards.

The strain government puts on marriage is horrific, and often the couple does not realize where the strain is coming from. Please, continually remind yourself that your enemy is not your spouse.

Your Friend Rick

---

1. "'American Dream' Proves Elusive...," *Wall Street Journal*, 29, 2024, p. A2.

More About How Your Schooling Affects Your Marriage

Letter 59

———— ✦ ————

D ear Robin,

Nationwide, the platoon schools were, and still are, heavily socialist, in their day-to-day regimentation, bureaucratic decision-making,[1] red tape, and especially their objective — which is to force the population into thinking socialist.

In other words, a child raised in a typical public school today isn't just *taught* to think socialist. He or she *lives* socialism's central planning, right out of the Soviet Gosplan playbook, every day.

Gosplan was the Union of Soviet Socialist Republics' central planning bureaucracy. It tried to own and control everything and everybody right down to the minutest detail, including what job you would do, how much you would be paid, where you would live, and what you would believe.

Possibly the most important fact in the health of your marriage is that, unless you were lucky, somewhere in your youth you were taught to think socialist, or you spent a lot of time in the company of people who were, or both.

Robin, your parents were not warned about this. Parents are not told the underlying messages taught to innocent children.

Equally important, practically no one is taught the opposite of socialism, meaning the System of Liberty. Liberty is not just a condition, it is a *system*, and these days I doubt one teacher in a thousand understands this, much less is equipped to teach about it.

In the mass-production-platoon schools of today, all the kids in a classroom are the same age.

Thirty kids the same age in a class is peer pressure on a grand scale.

Notice that when kids are not in school, you rarely see them in groups larger than six, and this is usually limited to sports.

Six is apparently the maximum group in which kids are comfortable, meaning they can rather easily say no and walk away if they do not agree with the group's behavior.

How many *adults* do you know who could comfortably walk away from a group of friends they regard as errant?

But the mass-production schools cram children together by the dozen.

Unless you were lucky, you have all that carefully engineered group-think embedded in your emotions. So some of your marital arguments may stem from the difference between the rate at which you and your spouse have been outgrowing them.

Especially if one of you clings tightly to those attitudes, while the other strives to escape them.

Very important: The science of psychology did not begin developing until the 20th century. Therefore, nearly all humans studied by psychologists and deemed within normal emotional parameters, are products of the mass-production, peer-pressure-cooker schools, which have swept the world.

I believe it may not be an exaggeration to say no one knows the characteristics of a "normal" person, because few of us have ever seen one, and those we have seen we probably dismissed as being weird.

Your Friend Rick

P.S. As I was writing this, it dawned on me that Sam and I had little interest in alcohol until we became teachers. Then ever since we resigned in the 1970s, we rarely touch the stuff.

---

1. Be sure to read "Government Schools: More Bureaucracy...," by Daniel Mitchel, *American Institute of Economic Research* website, Feb 18, 2021.

Counseling

Letter 60

———— ♦ ————

Dear Robin,

I have long been convinced much of the married population is carrying around heavy baggage from their childhoods, and in many cases, this baggage interferes with their marriages.

Sometimes the baggage has been created by the schools, and sometimes by the parents, or others.

I'm reluctant to blame parents. They are victims every bit as much as the children and teachers are. But some parents are just bad people. Vicious. Bullies.

For the first 13 years of our married life, Samantha and I did wonderfully. We grew constantly warmer, closer, and happier.

We lived in various places, all at least 400 miles from her parents.

Then they moved.

To less than 400 feet from us.

Within a year our marriage had gone on the rocks.

Again, one of the best pieces of advice I know to give is, **never let anyone invade your marriage**, not even your parents!

Perhaps another good way to put it is, never let the macro world invade your micro world.

We eventually began looking for a marriage counselor, and that helped a lot. She advised us to get out of Dodge, so we did, moving 300 miles away.

If you need that kind of help, one way to start searching for it is to ask your primary care physician for recommendations.

You might need to try several counselors before you find a good fit.

Again, Robin, nearly all parents were raised in the mass-production, peer-pressure-cooker schools. If yours botched their job as parents, this could be why.

Your Friend Rick

Set Your Marriage Free

Letter 61

———— ◆ ————

Dear Robin,

Neither of you is "normal." Almost no one is.

Like your parents and their parents before them, and their parents, etc., — including their teachers — you were probably raised in mass-production, peer-pressure-cooker schools, and are almost certain to be — wait for it — highly sensitive to peer pressure.

Do not let present or childhood peer pressure invade your marriage! All your behaviors, opinions, and responses, especially during an argument, should be *yours!* and not those of your acquaintances, from today or long ago.

Your spouse did not marry your peer group. Friends are not part of your marriage.

Work very hard at being an independent thinker charting your own course.

Remember this: One of the metrics schools use to judge a student's success or failure is popularity. If a student is a star, that is considered wonderful.

Again, Samantha and I were teachers, me for four years and her for eight. Between us, we have experience in all grades K-12, in middle-class American schools.

Of a popular child, we ask, what is he or she doing to be so popular with the mob?

And, what is a mob of kids qualified to judge?

Robin, when a child is in school, the parents are allowed to believe she or he is being raised by the teacher.

That's a lie.

Teachers are spread much too thin to give one-on-one attention to anyone except the troublemakers. And in many cases, when the teacher goes home for the evening, what occupies her or his thinking most is how to handle these rebels.

So, who is raising your child?

If it can't be the teacher, who is it?

The only other people your child spends much time with, in school, are the other children.

No one tells the parents this: kids in school are raised mostly by the other kids. It's why peer pressure is so dominating, so crushing, so overwhelming.

"Anyone taken as an individual is tolerably sensible and reasonable — as a member of a crowd, he at once becomes a blockhead."
— Fredrich Schiller quoted by Bernard Baruch in 1932.

That's from the highly entertaining and enlightening book, *Extraordinary Popular Delusions and the Madness of Crowds* by Charles McKay. I regard it as a must-read for every parent.

If you are not proud of some of the things you did as a teenager, you will see why.

In most cases, the movie industry is not on my list of heroes. But there's something they should be praised for. They were far ahead of the general public in sounding the warning about the peer pressure cooker schools.

Robin, after only one generation of children was raised in the platoon schools, which became widespread in the 1920s, movie makers saw something was terribly wrong. I suggest you watch the movies *Blackboard Jungle* (1955), *Rebel Without a Cause* (1955), *Lord of the Flies* (1963), and *To Sir with Love* (1967).

At the time in your life when you were experiencing the emotions and behaviors depicted in these films, you probably did not know what was happening to you. After all, your parents and the authorities sent you into these educational experiments because the experimenters had taught them it was the right thing to do.

But you are an adult now, and you have your eyes open. Do not let peer pressure near your marriage.

Your Friend Rick

Ladies, Is Your Man an Infantry Sergeant?

Letter 62

———— ✦ ————

D ear Robin,

What every successful military force in history has learned is that young males need good sergeants. Without good sergeants, young males are either helpless or dangerous, or both.

In civilian life, these "sergeants" might be athletic coaches, police officers, fire captains, scout leaders, fathers, uncles, or some other kind of top dog. They help young males mature.

This does not mean the "sergeant" needs to be a hardass all the time. But he should be always ready to jump into that role if needed.

A bigger part of a sergeant's job is to be a role model.

The most essential type of sergeant is the infantry sergeant. In a battle, his highly dangerous job is not so much to shoot back as to crawl from man to man, making sure everyone shoots back.

Infantry sergeants are made of mighty tough stuff — stuff that telegraphs to a woman, *I will never let you down. I will always be there for you. If necessary, I will kill or even die for you.*

I think coded into a woman's DNA is the desire to feel this assurance. She is designed to have babies. Late in her Stone Age pregnancies a woman was nearly helpless.

If I were a married woman, I would ask myself, is my man a sergeant?

Or does he still need to learn from one?

If he needs to learn, guess who has to do something about it?

The usual solution is to encourage him to spend time with men who are.

Your Friend Rick

Notes

Book One – Part 5

Arguments

Perspective

Letter 63

———— ✦ ————

D ear Robin,
  Always, always, always keep things in perspective.
No marriage is all sweetness and light. I suggest you try
developing this habit: When you feel an argument
coming on, the first thing that should pop into your head
is, *life is short.*

In fact, during a quiet, contemplative moment one day,
the two of you might agree that as soon as one feels a
quarrel erupting, he or she will have the responsibility of
asking out loud, "How important will this be a week or a
year from now, or when one of us is dead?"

Robin, after that question is asked, proceed with
the discussion, each trying to state his or her own
understanding of what the other is trying to say.

Once each has the other's agreement that, yes, that's
what I'm trying to tell you, then go on to debate the
merits of each other's facts and logic.

Do not have arguments. Have debates.

In the heat of the moment, it might also help to ask, are we trying to conquer each other, or just solve a problem?

If it is to solve a problem, what is the problem?

Agree on a description of it. Aim to have the attitude that you are two repairmen working as a team, not two warriors trying to defeat each other.

Bear in mind that emotions or hormones can easily torpedo attempts to be rational. What Samantha and I did when one or both were getting steamed was to table the argument until a day or two later.

Your Friend Rick

More About Arguments

Letter 64

———— ✦ ————

D ear Robin,

If an argument occurs, try to keep in mind the physical effects.

As anger builds, the heart beats faster, and blood pressure soars. This interferes with the brain's ability to process information. It can even literally reduce hearing, causing the words of the spouse to be misheard.

I have noticed many folks argue with emotion, not intelligence. Deep breathing helps change body and brain chemistry so a person can more easily return to logic and reason.

Also, never, never, never attack your spouse's self-esteem. Making someone feel bad about themselves is a bullying tactic, probably learned mostly in the schools, and then often brought home.

To understand the effect bullying can have on young people, note these statistics. In the decade after the advent of smartphones in 2007, the suicide rate among US adolescents rose 48%. For girls ages 10 to 14, it rose 131%.[1]

By the way, this is a good example of the extent to which mass-production, peer-pressure schools control a child's self-esteem.

Your Friend Rick

---

1. "End the Phone-based Childhood Now," *The Atlantic* website, March 13, 2024.

Apologies

Letter 65

———— ♦ ————

Dear Robin,

One way to keep arguments from becoming seriously painful is to always begin with an apology.

Even if your view is the right one — and of course it always is — a *sincere* "I'm sorry" helps grease the skids toward a resolution.

It delivers the message that *your mind is open* to hearing and seriously considering your mate's concern.

I remember a man long ago saying every morning when he awakens, he immediately says to his bleary-eyed wife, "I'm sorry."

When he began this practice, she'd ask, "What for?"

He'd say, "I don't know. But I'm sure that sometime today I will do something boneheaded, so I'm trying to lessen the impact."

To those who are not sure, yes, that's a joke — of the type that is funny because it reveals a perceived truth.

Again, sincerity is the key. In my opinion, an apology can be dimwitted, clumsy, even ridiculous. But as long as it is sincere, it will work.

Your Friend Rick

How to Prevent
an Argument

Letter 66

———— ◆ ————

Dear Robin,

In the entire 56 years of our marriage, Sam and I had uncountable disagreements. But I am pleased to say only one was a serious, enraged, shouting duel.

That argument lasted no more than an hour, but it certainly did hurt both of us and taught us never to let ourselves get that angry again.

Talk to a police officer, emergency room doctor, or a worker at a battered women's shelter. Serious physical injury is now common in marriages.

The reason Samantha and I managed to avoid the battles that seem standard among married folk these days is that we learned from that enraged example, and did the things that prevented a repeat. That is much of what Part Two, the *Owner's Manual* will be about.

Come to think of it, Robin, perhaps the most important marriage skill is how to disagree.

When I was learning how to make public appearances, I'd have a close friend critique me afterward.

He'd always start with two or three things I did well. This helped soften the blow when he got to the things I did badly.

That procedure transferred nicely to Samantha's and my marriage. Say something truly nice about your mate before you rip into him or her. After all, you are in love, right?

Arguments can be helpful if they are debates. But we must be careful to keep them from turning hurtful.

Do not try to hurt! Be a hair-trigger apologizer. As soon as you notice your loved one is upset, say you are sorry. At the moment, you may not know what you are sorry about, but you know emotional pain has been inflicted, and you never, ever want your lover to be in pain.

You may be entirely in the right, but being right is cold comfort when the love of your life is suffering.

Your mate needs to know her or his feelings are more important to you than your ego.

Apologies do not cost a cent, Robin, use them generously.

Sam and I found that before lodging a complaint, it helps to remind the other of how much you are in love with them. "I love you more than I can ever say. I do not have the words for how much you mean to me. We have a problem I'd like to talk about and bring up an agreement we made."

My suspicion is that in nearly every case of an argument, if you start by asking, "What did we agree to on this?," the answer will be, "We never made an agreement on it at all."

The follow-up should then be, "Let's wait a day or two until we cool down, then hammer out a procedure for this, and insert it in our written agreement."

Lots more on these written agreements in the *Owner's Manual.*

Your Friend Rick

Rules for Debate

Letter 67

———— ✦ ————

D ear Robin,
 Again, we found that whenever we got into a disagreement, as quickly as possible we should turn it into a debate.

You might do this by creating a double set of "Disagreement Cards" or "Rules for Debate." You might consider sitting down together and deciding which rules you will put on these cards.

Such rules can keep the outcome civil and productive instead of hurtful. As soon as one spouse feels things getting heated, that person should get out the cards.

Robin, you simply can't go wrong by beginning every complaint with the three magic words, "I love you."

"I love you more than I can say. You just ate the sandwich I was saving for my lunch."

"I love you more than anything. It's my turn to talk now."

"I love you tremendously. You promised to mow the lawn, and you didn't."

To get you started, here are a few suggestions for your Disagreement Cards.

1. No name-calling. **(I'm not Dufus, I'm Fred.)**

2. Define the issue at hand. **(As I see it, you agreed to take out the garbage yesterday and you didn't do it. Am I wrong?)**

3. No escalation; solve one problem at a time. **(You left the refrigerated groceries in the trunk and they got too warm. And by the way, you didn't wash the kitchen window or mow the lawn, and I saw you flirting with Chris.)** It's nearly impossible to respond calmly to an onslaught.

4. Feelings are monumentally important and must be respected, but they are not facts that can reveal what is right or true. When you sense an argument coming on, ask yourself, is this about my feelings, or the facts? If it is feelings, fine, but say so.

5. As soon as the disagreement begins, be ready to back down. No one is right 100% of the time.

Most importantly, again, always try to see things from your mate's point of view. Also, I suggest you keep this in mind: If you let a disagreement become a clash, then if you win, the person you dearly love loses.

Your Friend Rick

P.S. The 1970 movie *Love Story* became famous for the line, "Love means never having to say you're sorry."

This notion might be romantic but it is also insane. The person you love has feelings, and each of us is a fallible human. We make mistakes. In a marriage, the need to apologize is barely short of infinite. Better to do it too much than too little.

Again, apologies cost nothing, use them generously.

"Temper is what gets most of us into trouble. Pride is what keeps us there." — Mark Twain

Who Makes Your Decisions?

Letter 68

—————— ◆ ——————

D ear Robin,

I am sure you will avoid a great many arguments by making certain all your decisions are made by the two of you, not someone else.

The top decision of your married life is, will we have children, and if so how many?

And probably coming someday not far down the road, which sexes?

"But our parents want us to give them grandchildren," or something similar, should play no part in the discussion, much less the decision.

It's you, Robin, not someone else, who must live your life.

Your life is your property, and no one else's. You can make agreements or commitments, but you are no one's slave.

As mentioned earlier, the principle is called self-ownership. As far as I know, it was first taught by philosopher and physician John Locke (1632-1704). In the 20th century, self-ownership's most well-known advocate was probably economist Murray Rothbard (1926-1995).

The practical application of the self-ownership principle was famously expressed by philosopher and naturalist Henry David Thoreau (1817-1862): "If a man does not keep pace with his companions, perhaps it is because he hears a different drummer. Let him step to the music which he hears, however measured or far away."

So, who owns you?

You, and no one else, unless you voluntarily choose otherwise.

Your Friend Rick

P.S. Question: Who owns your marriage? Answer: Marriage is a partnership in the same way two business partners own a business. You need a written agreement that describes each person's rights and responsibilities. More about agreements in the *Owner's Manual*.

To Avoid Arguments, Organize Your Decision-Making

Letter 69

———————— ✦ ————————

Dear Robin,

Every human is different. We all have a different mix of needs, wants, desires, likes, dislikes, and opinions, all in a constant state of change.

Therefore, no matter how compatible we are with our spouses, we sometimes disagree. Samantha and I found that if we could not work out a win-win compromise, we were stuck with a win-lose compromise, or worse, lose-lose.

Usually, Robin, we'd talk it out and one would persuade the other. But on occasion, an issue would be so important to one or both that we could not compromise. We'd have a deadlock.

The way Samantha and I handled this is to divide up the final decision-making. When a deadlock occurred, one of us would be the final decider.

Crucially important: specify the final decider *before* the disagreements.

I suggest you set aside an hour or so one day soon to make a list of topics on which you as a couple make decisions. Then agree on the person who, in case of deadlock, will be the final decision-maker for each category.

Think in terms of bailiwicks (bale-ee-wicks). A bailiwick is a person's sphere of operations or area of responsibility.

Here is a sample of Samantha's and my list.

Bailiwicks

If we cannot agree on	The final decision-maker will be
Cars & car repairs	Rick
Choice of dentists	Samantha
Choice of doctors	Samantha
Choice of TV shows	Samantha
Clothing, Samantha's	Samantha
Clothing, Rick's	Samantha
Dog training	Rick
Content editing	Rick
Copy editing	Samantha
Defense of home & selves	Rick
Emergency supplies & equipment	Rick
Food	Samantha
Home decorating and organization	Samantha
Home repairs	Rick
Home safety	Rick
House cleaning	Samantha
Investments	Rick
Newsletter topics	Rick
Pharmaceuticals	Samantha
Tools & workshop	Rick
Vacation planning	Samantha

This is not to say *all* decisions were made by the designated spouse. The list came into play only when we could not agree, and compromise did not happen.

Robin, we found the more detailed the list, the fewer the deadlocks and arguments. Here's a possible reason why.

On any given issue, we'd know from the outset who would be the final decider in case of deadlock. So there was no reason to pursue the disagreement all the way to an eyeball-to-eyeball confrontation. The non-decider on that specific issue would already know who was the final decider, and would simply yield if deadlock appeared likely.

The sooner you make your list — *before* the next argument, instead of in the heat of battle — the more pain you will avoid.

An ounce of prevention is worth a pound of cure.

Here are more suggestions to make your system work smoothly.

• Make changes to the list any time, and check the whole list at least every 12 months.

• No change to the list can be made without both parties agreeing to it. (More about agreements in the *Owner's Manual.*)

• Each spouse should encourage the other to make a case for her or his view based on facts and logic.

• *Never* say, I don't want to hear it. If you love each other, always listen to each other.

• Never laugh at your partner's facts or logic. Listen respectfully.

• View an impasse as an opportunity to explore the other's mind to learn how she or he thinks. After all, you love this person, don't you want to understand her or him as fully as possible?

• The list is about decision-making, not the performance of duties. The decision maker might be one person, while the other does the work.

Again, this is not to say that on any given responsibility the designated decision-maker made all choices. This system comes into effect only in case of deadlock.

Who declared a deadlock?

I do not have an answer for that. In 56 years, we always both knew when a deadlock was near and there was no reason to pursue the matter further.

How to grease the skids and reduce hurt feelings? During any argument, both should repeatedly say something like, "I love you more than I can possibly say."

Again, turn arguments into debates. Here are rules for debate that might be helpful.

• A person must not shift her or his point of view. To do so is to begin a different and separate debate.

• Statements must be backed by evidence or reasons.

• Facts must be accurate.

Your Friend Rick

Money & Courting

Letter 70

———— ◆ ————

Dear Robin:

As far as I can tell, one of the points on which all marriage experts agree is, **never stop courting the person you love**.

The courting does not need to be expensive or elaborate, but it must be sincere.

Samantha adores flowers. When she and I were young and dirt poor, I could not afford to be a customer at flower shops. But I could stop by the roadside and gather a few well-chosen wildflowers.

Today we have lovely gardens with about a hundred rose bushes. I have two gardeners taking care of them.

Every few days I pick three fresh roses and make an arrangement for her. I keep it in the kitchen where she will see it most often.

Such gestures, or displays of affection, are mighty important, but they are not enduring. They must be continually renewed. Possibly the most powerful weapon that can easily destroy their value is money.

From what I have seen, in all too many cases one spouse produces the money income while the other produces the household labor income, and the household labor is considered of lesser value.

For instance, one drives to a job five days a week, while the other remains at home cooking, cleaning, shopping, paying bills, and performing all the other necessary duties the money-income earner does not.

When the latter wants or needs money, he or she must ask for it from the other, and the other decides how much will be doled out.

This control over the flow of the currency is a control on the life of the person.

Who feels good about being controlled?

I do not think the person who must always ask for the money — for the allowance — can be faulted for feeling like he or she is subservient to the other, or maybe even the other's slave.

Something to think about: to buy all the services continually or occasionally performed by a stay-at-home parent — cooking, cleaning, laundry, chauffeuring, pet care, minor repairs, nursing, etc. — the cost would be $178,201 per year.[1]

From day one, here is how Samantha and I handled the money for all our 56-year honeymoon. Any money income earned by either of us, no exceptions, went directly to her. Then to me, she doled out an agreed-upon amount, which I managed as joint savings and investments.

An absolute rule for 56 years was, above an agreed-upon amount, I was never permitted to make any movement of this capital without me explaining my thinking to her, and her giving consent.

Below that amount, she simply loved me and trusted my judgment. She kept our wallets topped up and paid all the bills.

For my personal cash or credit card spending, I was on my own below an agreed-upon amount. For her personal spending, I have no idea what she did. I knew she loved me, and I trusted her.

The general principle was, trust each other but bear in mind that we are human and humans make mistakes; when dealing with large sums, both should participate in the decision.

From day one, we never, ever had a disagreement over money, even when we were flat broke.

Your Friend Rick

P.S. Just FYI: For the first 26 years of our marriage, Sam earned far more money than I did, and for the remaining 30, our earnings ran about equal.

---

1. "How Much Is a Stay-at-Home Parent Worth?" *Investopedia* website, Apr 13, 2022.

Notes

Book One – Part 6

Starting Fresh

Profoundly Social (Contracts)

Letter 71

———— ✦ ————

Dear Robin,

Some of this letter may sound more complicated than it is. In fact, I suspect you have already worked out most of it through trial and error. Here we go.

Humans are profoundly social creatures. This is partly because of the need for specialization of labor and trade. (Let me emphasize partly. Love, comfort, safety, and other things are involved, too, but this letter is about the economics.)

Robin, if we all had to produce everything we need ourselves — all our food, clothing, shelter, automobiles, medical care, baseballs, clean water, and toenail clippers — few of us would survive, and these few would be unimaginably miserable.

I, for one, would not even know where to start to make these things for myself. Yet I have all of them.

Because each of us specializes in some kind of work and then trades our production for that of others. So we all live, many of us quite well.

The life force of this system is the contract or agreement.

If you will do this for me, I will do that for you.

Trade.

If you agree to give me the apple you worked hard to grow, I agree to give you the orange I worked hard to grow.

I agreed to give you 50 dollars in trade for the shirt you made. Then you used your 50 dollars to buy the pants Harry made.

In effect, I supplied the pants to you.

This is how a free economy — capitalism — works. We are all voluntarily agreeing to help each other even though in most cases we do not even know each other.

In each case, **we both receive something we value more than what we gave up. We both earn a profit. Otherwise, we would not go to the trouble of trading.**

Robin, the sum of all profits from all free trades, meaning ones in which there is no government interference, is what is called progress. It's how we got all the stuff we have. It's why we are not still living in caves, wearing bearskins, and fighting sabertooth tigers.

Before we go further, please note this: an economy is not a machine. It is an ecology, made of living, breathing organisms, meaning people. It's the most complex ecology on the planet by far.

Marriage is first and foremost the most important free trade we ever make. I agree to do an endless number of things for you if you agree to do an endless number of things for me.

Robin, I doubt any couple gets their first try at the agreement perfect. But an agreement, or contract, can be changed with the consent of both parties.

A crucial point: our entire civilization is the result of agreements, of contracts. That's how humans organize themselves.

In your pre-nuptial agreement, you may want to insert a clause committing to revisit it at regular intervals.

What, you don't have a prenup? No problem. Start writing a postnup. The *Owner's Manual* will help you devise it.

In it, promise each other that in the first year, you will revisit and revise it every three months. After that, maybe every six months, and then perhaps annually.

Again, an agreement, or contract, can be changed with the consent of both parties.

A handy rule of thumb might be, if you are having unpleasant disagreements more than once per month, one or both of you should suggest a revisit of the related parts of the agreement.

If your agreement does not cover something, write a clause that does.

By the way, are you the kind of person who has your car regularly tuned up, as opposed to just buying a new one every few months? Me, too.

If you can find a marriage counselor agreeable to you both, going in for a marriage tune-up every six months or a year might be a good idea.

As with your car, don't wait for something to break down. Have a regularly scheduled maintenance visit. A stitch in time...

Your Friend Rick

P.S. Here is perhaps the most important discovery Samantha and I ever made:

Arguments can be superb diagnostic tools. In almost all cases, an argument was a sign that we had neglected to write down an agreement about something important to one or both of us.

The Marriage Ceremony

Letter 72

————— ✦ —————

D ear Robin,
Marriage ceremonies have always baffled me.
For one thing, in the traditional version, the vows —
meaning the agreements, the contracts — only consume
a minute or two, and are ridiculously unclear. They may
be something like, "I take thee to be my lawful wedded
wife/husband, to have and to hold from this day forward,
for better or worse, for richer or poorer, in sickness and in
health, to love and cherish, until death do us part."

That's it? That's supposed to cope with decades
and decades of uncertainties, contingencies, mistakes,
disagreements, and catastrophes?

That's not an agreement, Robin, it's wishful thinking.
It's romance, hearts, and flowers, a diversion from the
seriousness, the full meaning of what is happening.

I am delighted that couples today are writing their own
vows. But I have yet to see a *ceremony* in which there was
an attempt to honor what is really going on.

To my mind, the marriage ceremony should be
secondarily about romantic music, flowing gowns, gifts,
cake, flower petals, or dancing. It's okay if these are
included, of course, but they are not the primary purpose
of the ceremony.

Primarily it should be about the *contract*! The *prenup*!
The *agreement*!

This is what we will do *for* each other, and what we
won't do *to* each other.

I am not saying the prenup should be read in full before
the spectators. For that purpose, I am sure a preamble of
no more than fifty words would suffice.

But the ceremony should be designed so that everyone
attending — especially the young unmarrieds — will
know the most important agreement of the couple's life
is being put into effect.

One way to do this might be for the couple and person
officiating to meet at the altar where there is a podium
holding the prenup in its heavy, sturdy case. (Heavy
signifying this is a serious matter.)

The officiate says her or his introduction.

Then, in my opinion, with solemnity, the officiate
draws the agreement from its case and invites the parties
to sign.

After it is signed by each of the three, the rings
are exchanged to symbolize that the agreement is now
binding and in effect.

Once this shared commitment is solemnized, fun and romantic parts of the ceremony and celebration could then commence.

Your Friend Rick

Beware of Handshake Deals

Letter 73

———— ✦ ————

D ear Robin,

In my opinion, one of the most crucial mistakes in life that nearly everyone makes is handshake deals between close friends.

A handshake deal is an agreement or contract that is not written or in some other way recorded and saved.

Friends tend to make handshake deals, trusting each other to perform. It makes things happen more quickly.

For instance, if you and I agree to meet at 5:30 pm at the corner of 6th and Main, we would not likely go to the trouble of writing and signing two copies of our agreement.

For matters that are trivial, handshake deals are fine. But for things we regard as serious, they are poison. I have seen a great many friendships blow up because the parties made an important commitment without putting it in writing. Each thinks she or he remembers correctly what was said, and neither is willing to back down, so the friendship ends.

The problem is that as life goes on, conditions change and distractions pile up, while no one has a perfect memory.

Also, the parties often were not "on the same page" in the first place.

The upshot is that molehills become mountains, and the friendship fails.

The more important a friend is to us, the more careful we should be about our agreements.

The traditional marriage ceremony is a handshake deal.

If, when you married you went down the handshake road, my suggestion is to reverse course by creating a post-nuptial agreement in writing.

Your Friend Rick

Get Remarried

Letter 74

———— ◆ ————

D ear Robin,
   Thanks for your question about our marriage ceremonies. Samantha and I were married four times.

The first was in a church in Fullerton, California; the second in another church in Placentia, California; the third on the Love Lock Bridge in Paris; the fourth on the beach at Ragged Point on Highway 1 in California, a truly spectacular spot with high cliffs above crashing waves.

Why four times? Because we're in love.

You might want to carefully examine every part of your agreement, revising whatever is necessary, and then celebrating.

Samantha and I wanted to formally declare to each other that our marriage remained healthy, strong, and fully in effect, meaning our agreement was still alive and well, and both of us were 100% behind it.

In other words, each marriage was a... (next letter)

Your Friend Rick

...Fresh Start

Letter 75

———— ♦ ————

Dear Robin,

Even if you have been married for decades, it never hurts to make a fresh start.

Part of doing this is to explore each other's minds.

Nobody stays the same. You have both been changing. So get to know your spouse more completely, especially in regard to his or her thoughts about marriage.

You might be pleasantly surprised at what you have been missing.

A way to begin doing this can be to discuss topics you may have never before explored together, just as when you first met.

Robin, if you aren't into art, for instance, give it a try. Same for astronomy, geology, music, child-rearing, cooking, and a host of other topics.

To Samantha and me, there is almost no subject unworthy of exploration. Two of her favorites are art and architecture, which she introduced to me. I'm grateful.

In short, if you want your lover to stay interested in you, cultivate a mind he or she finds interesting.

After all, is it your spouse's bones, muscles, and skin you are in love with, or his or her mind?

A *Wall Street Journal* article, "The Secret to Lasting Romance? Doing New Things Together,"[1] reports that psychological studies show, "Simply sharing new experiences and activities increases physical desire in long-term partnerships."

Further, "Here the research is clear: Self-expression isn't simply a luxury of youthful courtship but an essential feature of any satisfying long-term relationship."

Also, "these effects extend to the bedroom, too. ...couples who saw their partners as sources of insight, excitement, and new experiences had more desire for sex with each other. Simply sharing new experiences and activities increased physical desire."

You might want to take a look at *The Great Courses* by The Teaching Company (1-800-832-2412, thegreatcourses.com). Samantha and I have been through scores of them and found almost all enlightening and even entertaining.

But beware of the economics and finance courses. There are two general economic paradigms in the world today, the Austrian and the Keynesian (Canes-ee-an), which is a type of socialism.

Governments use Keynesian, so this is what is taught in almost all schools and colleges. But in my opinion, the much more politically realistic paradigm is the Austrian, of Nobel Prize winners Friedrich Hayek and James Buchanan.

Here is a possible list of six thought adventures you might enjoy exploring together. They may be deeper and more revealing than any you have ever before experienced, so expect to delve into them many times.

• Do you believe you have a spirit (or soul) that will outlive your body? Another way to ask this is, do you believe that when you die, that's the end, finished, kaput forever? Or is there a hereafter?

• If you believe in a hereafter, does this belief affect your day-to-day behavior?

• If you don't believe in a hereafter, does this affect your behavior?

• If you have a spirit, during bedroom intimacy does it participate, or does it go on a coffee break? In other words, is the intimacy just a physical act, a recreation, with little or no emotion — is it just a way to satisfy hormonal urges? Is there more happening, on a higher plane?

• If your spirit does not go on a break, and if more goes on emotionally, spiritually, psychologically, or in some other way — how long can the bonding from the intimacy last? An hour? A week? A lifetime?

• Can a couple deliberately break the bond, or does it have a mind of its own? Would it last even if they did not want it to?

Your Friend Rick

---

1. By David Robson, May 11-12, 2024, *Review* p. C4.

Our Old-Fashioned Marriage

Letter 76

———— ✦ ————

Dear Robin,

Aside from finding each other, probably the most fortunate part of our marriage is that when we got married in 1967, both at age 20, we were virgins. Although it was a close-run thing.

We were and will forever remain thankful to have completely bypassed the sexual revolution and all its numerous mental and emotional illnesses.

In our "old-fashioned" marriage, we were easily able to *bond!* and stay that way. I am totally confident neither of us ever fell victim to temptation.

What can you do if you were not so fortunate as to escape the sexual revolution?

We cannot undo what is done. But I think a must for a fresh start would be to insert in your marriage contract the ancient promise that was once common in wedding vows: "I pledge thee my troth."

This is a formal, public way of saying, I promise to remain faithful to you, and to you only, in bedroom activities.

Or, from this day forward, we are one flesh.

In your contract, you might also insert a short sentence: "I promise to do all I can to avoid comparing you with others."

More about contracts and their importance in the *Owner's Manual.*

By the way, in suggesting you consider building an old-fashioned marriage, I do not think I am suggesting any measures that cannot be undone. So I hope you will give old-fashioned a try, and if it does not work for you, experiment with something you believe might work better.

And that would be...?

I have no idea.

Your Friend Rick

Our 95% Guideline

Letter 77

———— ◆ ————

Dear Robin,

When trying to figure out how to spend an evening, or do something else with our spare time, what Samantha and I must have said to each other a thousand times was, "Just being together is 95% of everything."

Now that Sam is on the other side, the truth of this to me is breathtaking. I feel an enormous gratitude that we both always stuck to our "95% Guideline."

Robin, as long as we were within touching distance, that was enough.

Just sitting thousands of times on park benches, holding hands, and talking about any number of fascinating subjects, is a large part of why I can still feel Samantha with me today. Her thoughts became mine, and vice versa, and I often knew what she was going to say before she said it. And still do.

In short, do not — I repeat, do *not* — become boring.

When Samantha graduated from college, she was burned out. She hated the thought of reading anything.

But after five years or so of watching me read —
meaning watching me read things I *chose* to read, instead
of being forced to, as in school — she got the bug and
never turned back.

It's called research. But what it really is, is exploration.
Armchair travel. Together. When I recall doing it, I miss
it so much it hurts.

The more you armchair travel, the more interesting you
are, not only to your partner but to yourself. Neither of us
was ever bored, with the other or alone.

I have been told that in the restaurants we frequented
for lunch, the staff would enjoy watching our habit of
holding hands across the table, eye-to-eye, and rapt with
each other's observations, opinions, and insights.

If you want your spouse to stay interested in you, stay
interesting. One of Samantha's favorite T-shirts says, "I
read, so I know things."

Your Friend Rick

P.S. I wonder if one reason humans are supposed to
mate is to delight in armchair travel together.

I do know this. During summers after dark, Sam
and I would sit side-by-side holding hands in lounge
chairs on the front driveway. Using stabilized ten-power
binoculars, we would gaze at the Milky Way, planets, and
stars, and teach each other what we had learned in our
studies about them.

We still do that, and we cover many other subjects, too. But now anything lengthy is difficult for her.

More than I can ever express, I look forward to being with her again, so she can teach me more.

Memories

Letter 78

———— ♦ ————

D ear Robin,

When we were in our mid-fifties we lived near California's Napa Valley. It was one of our favorite places to explore.

One day we were visiting wineries and stopped for a break in a grove of huge trees with a gravel parking lot.

The place was deserted, and we were standing beside the car stretching our legs.

One of us, I don't remember which, took the opportunity to steal a kiss.

Intimately wrapped in each other's arms, we were slow to notice the sound of gravel crunching. Too late, we realized a school bus had pulled in and parked about ten feet away.

From above, the crowd looking down at us was shouting, "Look at the old people making out!"

We were afraid we'd be arrested for corrupting a busload of minors, but we got away cleanly. Apparently, no one thought to get our license number.

It's one of our best memories.

But most of our remembrances are not accidental. We planned them.

To a large extent, I believe, a 56-year honeymoon is built on reminiscing, on sharing recollections. Sam often said, "Life is about gathering memories."

Her favorite way of introducing a suggestion that we go out and do something new was, "Let's go make a memory."

Everyone has heard the cliché, "Life is short." I didn't realize how short until her passing. I now have endless memories of days decades ago that seem like they were just weeks ago.

Indeed, Robin, sometimes our 56 years seem like 56 days.

Keep your memories alive and strong. Visit them often. Do not let them fade. Someday they will be the most valuable things you have.

Thank you so much, Sam, our memories are a comfort.

Your Friend Rick

Dating

Letter 79

—————— ✦ ——————

D ear Robin,
     Remember when you were courting, you made
practically everything a date. Even when preparing for a
trip to the grocery store, you'd spruce up a bit and fantasize
about soon meeting your sweetheart.

For the second half of our 56-year marriage, Samantha
and I lived that way day-to-day.

We had finally been able to engineer our work lives to
enable us to work together nine to five. We usually ran
errands together and had lunch together.

Each little journey was a minor special occasion we'd
prepare for as if we were still wooing each other.

In other words, we knew the day would come when we
would not be together, so we treasured each opportunity to
connect. Nothing fancy, but special never the less.

Please, do not stop courting your loved one.

Your Friend Rick

P.S. Right from the beginning, Robin, when we were dirt poor, I made it a habit to bring Samantha wildflowers. We couldn't afford store-bought.

After we hit pay dirt, I still brought her flowers, even though she had about a hundred rose bushes of numerous colors.

She brought me flowers, too. I miss that terribly.

Facial Hair, Makeup & Arguments

Letter 80

———— ◆ ————

Dear Robin,

In the 1980s and '90s, Samantha was one of the most successful salespeople for a Fortune 500 corporation. At the time she quit to work for our company, Henry Madison Research, Inc., she was selling million-dollar contracts. This was at a time when a million was a lot of money.

The company had a strict policy against salesmen having facial hair.

They'd found that the less of the salesman's face was visible, the less he was trusted by customers.

On the female side of the trust issue, I once knew a woman who regarded herself as unattractive, so she wore heavy makeup. Sometimes it was so thick and extensive friends would not recognize her if passing her in a hallway.

I have long wondered if difficulty in seeing a person's face can interfere with a marriage.

Robin, no marriage is 100% bliss, so we all have occasional arguments. Distrust can easily rachet a small spat up into an emotional, or even physical battle.

In any marriage, therefore, it is essential that both parties be convinced that the other would *never* lie to them.

I suspect it is in our DNA that during a disagreement, both parties consciously or unconsciously try to read the face of the other, to be confident the other is not shading the facts.

Let me emphasize, I believe attempting to read the other's expression is automatic, we may not even know we are doing it. We just know intuitively that more information is better than less.

You might try this experiment: reduce the facial hair and makeup, and see if the severity of the arguments diminishes.

Also, obviously, we *want* to be able to trust our mates, and vice versa.

Trust once lost is almost impossible to regain.

So I think your marriage agreement should include a clause declaring something like, I will never, ever lie to you under any circumstances.

And please, do not get cute about it. Be a straight shooter. Say what you regard as the exact truth, without loopholes.

Loopholes make the trust go away.

Your Friend Rick

I'd Still Choose You

Letter 81

———— ♦ ————

Dear Robin,

On her nightstand, Samantha kept a small candle. In fact, I still have it, on my nightstand.

It has an inscription. "If I could choose again, I'd still choose you."

It's a sweet sentiment, but it does not carry the weight it should.

Samantha and I actually did choose each other — 20,468 times.

Actions speak louder than words. Each morning we'd roll out of bed and proceed to spend another 24 hours as a married couple.

We always had the choice not to do so. Any morning, one or both of us could have decided, "I am not doing this anymore, goodbye."

But we never did. Never even came close. For 20,468 mornings, we chose to stay together.

If I were counseling a young couple, I would tell them, "You are not the property of your loved one. You are not a slave. You can walk away."

So each day you decide to stay with your spouse, your decision is a repeat of the commitments you made at the altar. You are, in fact, remarrying each day.

Robin, perhaps it would be a good idea to form a habit. Upon waking each morning, kiss and say, "I love you and I'm staying."

Your Friend Rick

Flirting

Letter 82

———— ✦ ————

D
ear Robin,

When it comes to the opposite sex, men are almost uncontrollably sight-oriented.

It's an old silent movie cliché but I have done it. Strolling down a street and passing a beautiful woman, I've walked into telephone poles.

What is the difference between flirting and teasing? I don't know, so I am using two Apple Dictionary definitions:

- Flirting is to behave as though attracted to or trying to attract someone, but for amusement rather than with serious intentions.

- Tempt (someone) sexually with no intentions of satisfying the desire aroused.

I like the second one best.

Inside marriage, flirting is great, because "no intentions" can easily turn into "intentions," and that's good for the marriage.

Outside marriage, what's the point?

As a high school teacher, I often witnessed young women dressing alluringly and flirting with the boys, and with the male teachers.

Men are saturated with testosterone. They don't choose to be, but they are.

Why some women try to trigger the hormone and emotions, I do not know.

I do know some people like power. They enjoy manipulating others, using them as puppets. Maybe that's what flirting is about. It's the first step toward a career in politics.

Of course, lots of men flirt, too. Same question. Why?

I'm convinced there are people who get some kind of sick thrill out of stimulating a person and then walking away. It's like tying a tin can to a dog's tail. It's cruel.

It might be okay if we could know the hidden feelings of our targets. But we can't. Will they take this apparent interest seriously?

My advice to any woman: no teasing unless you intend to deliver the goods. In that case, it's not teasing, it's an offer, the first step in a contract, which we will explore shortly.

"But I have a *right* to dress as I please!" I can hear some exclaim, and this is 100% true. You own yourself. Your body

is your property to do with as you please. After all, if you
don't own you, who does?

As I see it, if you want, you have every right to walk around
naked on the waterfront at 3:00 am. But if you do, it will
likely catch up to you.

In the company of a flirt, most guys will control
themselves, but some won't, and you never know who they
are. I know a woman who flirted a lot, and it caught up to
her.

In short, for males and females alike, when flirting, **there
is just no way to know what is being triggered in the
mind of the other person.**

Except probably between wife and husband. In that case,
go for it!

And if you are a guy, look out for telephone poles.

Your Friend Rick

Fashion, Math & Health

Letter 83

————— ✦ —————

Dear Robin,

Look out for the fashion industry.

Granted, some of these people are wizards at making you look attractive, but I suspect many more are wizards at making money.

They cook up whatever they think they can call the latest fashion while pushing the idea that "fashionable" and "attractive" are synonyms. If you are not adorned with the latest and greatest hot new thing, you aren't attractive.

This ties your magnetism to your money.

Robin, scientific research has shown in every culture, good looks are mostly a matter of clear skin and mathematical ratios, meaning the number of millimeters between one facial part and another.

In other words, not surprisingly, a set of ratios generally felt to be attractive is also an indicator of good health.

The ratios are not an exact science, but you will find an article about them titled, "The Ideal Face and

Profile: Here's What Mathematics Says About Beauty" at plasticsurgerycal.com.

For instance, under the "Golden Ratios" theory, the distance from the top of a woman's nose to the center of her lips should be 1.618 times the distance from the center of her lips to her chin.

Under the "Theory of Vertical Fifths," the distance between the tip of her nose and the skin overlaying the levator labii superioris muscle should be equal to the nose's width.

Further, it is my opinion that women are more interested in romance when they feel good about themselves. And this, too, is in the DNA. To be able to produce and raise healthy children, she must be in good health, and indicators of beauty are also those of good health.

Does this apply to men? Yes, in men, too, indicators of attractiveness are indicators of good health.

But as for a male's libido, I could be wrong of course, but I think this is almost entirely dependent on how many gallons of testosterone he's hauling around.

I hope it is obvious I believe there is way, way too much emphasis on looks. I know people for whom it is an obsession that controls their lives.

In my opinion, if you are healthy, friendly, hardworking, and honorable, and you smile and *have interesting things to say!*, you are well on your way to being stunning.

Samantha cheers this remark by actress Naomi Watts: "There's only one you. Stay away from the trends. Be you. And don't be afraid of that."[1]

Summarizing, I have always found that following the crowd is a sure route to stupidity and embarrassment. Perhaps one of the best examples is the sack dresses of the 1950s. Considered highly fashionable — the latest! — they were made from burlap bags. Online, you might find a photo of movie star Marilyn Monroe wearing a potato bag.

Your Friend Rick

P.S. To me it is astonishing how powerful these mathematical ratios can be. While working on this letter, I had occasion to encounter a young woman in Army uniform. She wore no makeup, no fancy clothes. All strictly military. But she had a mathematically perfect face, of which I have only seen perhaps a half-dozen in my life.

I am 77, and my body no longer has the foggiest idea what a testosterone molecule looks like. But she smiled, and I was paralyzed.

Honestly, I could not move. I just stood there staring, with my jaw at full drop. My I.Q. sunk to 12, and if I'd been young, with a full load of testosterone, I'd probably have gone into convulsions.

I am sure every heterosexual guy reading this knows what I am talking about.

Here is a possible antidote to this extremely primitive automatic knee-jerk response system. View the human face, body, and skin not as a toy to be acquired and played with, but as a communication device, like a telephone, for making the most profound connection you will ever experience.

Even if, like Samantha and me, you are way, way over the hill, you still have all that skin, which can evoke breathtaking pleasures.

Again, a communication device.

---

1. "Naomi Watts Wants Menopause To Be The New Puberty," *Wall Street Journal,* Review, June 29, 2024, p.c14.

Loving Her Spirit

Letter 84

———— ♦ ————

Dear Robin,
   Perhaps a decade ago I stumbled onto a unique painting of a woman.

It grabbed my imagination. Wrapped in a simple white Native American blanket with matching headband, this heart-stopper stands ankle-deep at the shore of a lake, with the sunset at her back.

The artist was clever. Nearly all of the woman's face is in shadow, rather ethereal and difficult to see. This enables the viewer's imagination to fill in with any face he wishes.

I, of course, have always envisioned Samantha's.

My personal title for the painting is *Samantha's Spirit*.

For ten years the image has hung in our kitchen so it can draw my attention several times a day.

The painting's importance to me is that it depicts the parts of Samantha that I love most — her personality, her spirit, and her heart.

And her laugh. Robin, at age 76, she still enjoyed life so much that her chuckle had a vivacity that would pass for that of a 30-year-old.

Anyone who knew her well could give you a long list of her spirit's admirable traits. For starters: gentle, curious, wise, kind, affectionate, explorative, aware, caring, and logical. The painting conveys this, a special person.

Here is a suggestion. Find a picture you can use to depict your lover's spirit and hang it where you will see it often.

It need not be a picture of a person. Among her friends, Sam is often described as their Rock of Gibraltar. One of her own descriptions of herself is of a soaring owl hauling away a basket of other people's troubles.

Most importantly, I made sure Samantha occasionally noticed me gazing upon the picture — upon her spirit.

Your Friend Rick

What Love Is like on Samantha's Side

Letter 85

————— ✦ —————

D ear Robin,

Tonight on the veranda, as we gazed west, Samantha and I were watching a breathtaking sunset, and conversing, as we did whenever possible till she passed to her new location.

I asked, "Can I have a better description of what your side is like."

She has often done her best to tell me but without much success. Tonight, however, was her best try yet. Here's the story.

Samantha has often reminded me that, "You and I are now one spirit."

She tells me she resides in my solar plexus, which is the site of a lot of human electrical activity. (Didn't know anything about the solar plexus or its electrical equipment till she told me to "look it up!")

She has previously gotten across to me that on her side, intimacy between lovers is constant and wonderful, but not so intense as love-making here.

Tonight we batted the idea around a bit more, and she finally came up with this explanation: "Of course, you aren't here, so I have not experienced it yet. But as I am told, the constant closeness on my side is not like an orgasm."

She went on, "It is the afterglow. But it never stops. I'm sure we'll know more when you get here."

Right now, although we are separated, she *feels it a bit*. When I finally am there, she says, "I'm told the afterglow will be full strength."

She adds, "I suppose it's valid to say that on earth, afterglow is a taste of heaven."

My job requires me to be a professional skeptic. But there is one thing of which I have become totally certain: there is a spiritual aspect to bedroom intimacy, and it is not trivial.

Your Friend Rick

Mixed Group Conversations

Letter 86

———— ✦ ————

Dear Robin,

When I was a fledgling teacher, the teachers' lunch room was always divided between male tables and female tables.

After a few weeks, one of the women invited me to sit at their table of eight.

Hmmm. One man. Eight women. That's the kind of invitation I never, ever turn down.

Some of the men would glare daggers at me as if I were a traitor. But I'd been shot at with real bullets enough that it did not bother me in the least.

The women just sort of forgot I was a guy and quickly adopted me as one of the girls. So, for years I went where no man has gone before.

Each lunch hour I got to sit in on fascinating conversations about menstruation, orgasms, flirting, crying, giving birth, men, and every other kind of female concern.

Yes, guys, they really are from a different planet, and it must be a captivating place.

This brings me to mixed group conversations.

Robin, throughout my life it's been my experience that in mixed get-togethers, the men tend to dominate. I don't know why. Perhaps they are louder, or more competitive.

Or maybe women tend to be inclusive, while men, suffering from testosterone poisoning, want to be exclusive, leaders of the pack.

In any case, I have often observed women being left out, purposely sidelined, even shouted down, and ridiculed, as if their viewpoints are childish.

When Samantha and I were in a mixed group, I never permitted it. I did not say anything about it, I just kept asking her and any other women for their views.

One of the most outrageous things I ever witnessed happened at an investment conference where I was speaking. After my appearance, I was in the hallway with a group gathering around to ask questions. As a young man and woman approached, I saw him lean over to her and command, "Now don't *say* anything!"

So I kept all my remarks directed at her.

Guys, if you want to be a hero to your lover, make sure she is invited into your conversations. She does not need to accept, but she does need to know she is not being pushed out.

Your Friend Rick

Guys, Here Is What Women Find Sexy

Letter 87

———— ✦ ————

Dear Robin,

Thanks for your letter asking for a possible connection between the intellect and the bedroom.

My answer is, I do not know of any scientific study on the question, but here's an anecdote that might shed some light on it.

Liberty is not just a condition, it is a system. I am one of the few people in the world who specialize in understanding the System of Liberty[1] well enough to earn his living writing and speaking about it, to try to help rescue what is left of it.

Sometimes a group of us meet at a resort area such as Aspen, Colorado to spend a few days with like-minded friends.

During a break at one such meeting long ago, I was part of a mixed group of men and women. I asked the women something like, "Do you find that men in this System of Liberty business treat you differently than other men do?"

I expected a few quiet moments in which the women would mull it over and come up with a thoughtful answer.

Instead, there was an instantaneous and loud, "Oh yes! You *listen* to us!"

The women went on to explain that most men only pretend to be listening to women. They give a woman a few moments to express her thoughtful opinion, then blow right by it as if she isn't even in the room.

Robin, the discussion continued, but for me the main lesson that shook out of it was, **a woman finds it sexy when a man shuts his mouth and makes a genuine effort to absorb her words.**

Your Friend Rick

P.S. After that lesson, every few months I would ask Samantha, "Have I been listening to you closely enough lately?" I am proud to say, she never said no.

---

1. Probably the first to coin a term that assumed liberty is a system was Adam Smith in his 1776 book *Wealth of Nations.*

Snide Remarks

Letter 88

———— ✦ ————

Dear Robin,

In case you have not guessed by now, there is nothing that makes me more angry than the mistreatment of a woman. I go ballistic.

It has been my experience that many men when in the company of an all-male group, make snide remarks about their wives.

These guys apparently assume there is some sort of male code that prevents such comments from getting back to their mates.

I suspect they are right about that male code, but not always. It only takes one man to spill the beans. He goes home and tells his wife, sister, mother, cousins, or maybe all of them, and they spread it to who knows where.

Robin, his wife may never say anything about it, but I simply cannot imagine her emotional pain.

It could be so great that in some cases, snide remarks are the first step on the road to divorce.

Do women do this, too? I think so, and Sam says yes, but doesn't venture to know how much.

Of this I am certain. People love to gossip. Please, never say anything negative about your loved one unless you want the whole world to hear it.

Your Friend Rick

Opposite Sex Friendships

Letter 89

———— ♦ ————

Dear Robin,

This part of the marriage agreement is of major importance. A lot of careful thought should go into this question:

"Is it okay for one or both of you to have deep friendships with members of the opposite sex?"

As for me, I was apparently born with self-control made of carbide steel. Despite a category four level of testosterone poisoning, plus some mighty powerful temptations, I always stayed true to Sam.

I was never seriously inclined to touch another woman in a romantic or sexual way. Sam absorbed everything I had to give.

There are exceptions, but in general, I do not think women have as much trouble with erotic temptation as men do. They have a lot less of that treacherous hormone — between a tenth and a twentieth of the male load.

So, the trust a woman needs to marshal to be comfortable about her husband's close friendships with other women is probably about the size of Jupiter. But I am not a woman, I'm just guessing.

I do know I've seen a lot of marriages demolished by unchecked testosterone.

If Samantha had vetoed my close female friendships, I would have understood completely and complied. But despite knowing I was drenched in that wicked toxin, she never did.

By the way, Robin, over the years, I have seen a great many female-female relationships that looked to me as if they were really marriages except, as far as I know, they stopped at the bedroom door. Often they were two mothers living together.

For any close and warm relationship between two or more people — and even those not so close and warm — many of the suggestions in this book can apply, especially those in Book Two, the *Owner's Manual*, which we will begin now.

Your Friend Rick

P.S. A surprise in my life since Samantha's passing is that I not only never stop loving her, I love her more every day.

Throughout our marriage, if she was ever jealous of my friendships with other women, I never saw it. She always knew she owned my heart — lock, stock, and barrel — and I was happy about that.

Most importantly, she and other women knew she could always trust me to keep my promises.

Trust. It's crucial. More about it coming up.

By the way, I wonder if you could do us a favor. What hurts us most is, not being able to touch each other. So for us, please touch your loved one every chance you get.

In other words, you have skin, please use it.

Notes

Book Two

The Owner's Manual

Ethics & The 17-Word Solution

◆

The two rules that make all good things in civilization possible, including warm, strong marriages, as well as relationships in business, friendship, employment, and your neighborhood.

Published with the permission of Ethics Solutions®

Dear Reader,

In achieving whatever it is you want from your life, your marriage will be either a headwind or a tailwind.

Earlier, I wrote that this book is actually two books.

People seem to absolutely *love* Book One and want to know how to have a marriage with so much affection, joy, and contentment. They commonly say they can't wait to tell their friends about it.

Obviously, Samantha's and my marriage has been a strong tailwind, and we hope you enjoy the same.

However, although you may come away from Book One with an inspiring picture of your new *goal*, you don't yet know how we produced it or, more importantly, once you have it, how to *preserve* it!

So, this book — Book Two — is the how-to.

It will necessarily be less entertaining because it is literally an *Owner's Manual*. It describes the nuts and bolts of *how* to operate a marriage day-to-day.

In short, Book One is lots of fun, but the *Owner's Manual* is the real prize.

It will pay off for you over and over for the rest of your life. Samantha and I are the voices of experience.

Trust

Letter 90

───────── ♦ ─────────

Dear Robin,

Ethics is the basic rules of conduct that make it possible for humans to live and work together.

Let me emphasize, living together. Probably the most important glue that holds a marriage together is ethics. I think it is even more important than bedroom intimacy.

In my opinion, if you can't *trust* your loved one, you married the wrong person and your life is probably awful, or will be.

This *Owner's Manual* is a collection of excerpts from my ethics handbook published in 2015. The handbook was originally written to train employees and educate children. But these passages from it have been extracted and revised to help married couples or those planning to marry.

I am doing this because experience has convinced me beyond the shadow of a doubt that the more you understand and use the 17-Words — which are:

Do all you have agreed to do and,
do not encroach on other persons or their property

— all your relationships will be improved. Every aspect of your life will go more smoothly, and most importantly your marriage.

The 17-Words are, more than anything else, a prevention, a way of heading off trouble before it can develop. As Benjamin Franklin wrote in *Poor Richard's Almanac*, "A stitch in time saves nine."

Your Friend Rick

Your Reputation

Letter 91

———— ♦ ————

Dear Robin,

Please take my word for it. For a warm, loving, and successful marriage, nothing is more important than careful ethical reasoning. It is easy, but almost no one these days is taught how to do it, or even how to recognize ethics when they see it. That's what my ethics handbook is designed to cure.

So let's get started.

There is an expression usually used jokingly: "Your better half."

It means that when you marry, the two of you become a single person, and your spouse is the better half.

It is not a precise fact, of course, but it reflects a truth. Like it or not, you are a team now, and when your spouse says or does something good or bad, you share the credit or the blame.

Getting married meant the world stopped asking, what kind of person is she or he and began asking, what kind are they?

You may not want it, but you are stuck with it. This means you need to pay attention not only to your own ethics but those of your spouse too.

In other words, one of the many things you were signaling when you got married was that you approve of your lover's behavior.

Robin, the best way I know to make this melding of your reputations work for both of you is to learn to *think* like a 19th century Common Law lawyer. This skill is what you are about to learn.

If that goal sounds daunting, do not worry. I will make it easy for you.

Unlike in political law today, ethics was embedded in the venerable Common Law (which for our purposes can also be called Natural Law). We will pull it out and study it.

You might be thinking, "Oh my gosh, I can't do that! Law is way, way over my head!"

Granted, today's *political* law is way, way over your head, because it is way, way over everyone's head, including the people who make it up.

The Federal Code of Regulations alone — which does not include the thousands of state and local laws — is 165,000 pages, takes up 27 feet of shelf space, and includes about 300,000 laws.[1]

In other words, the ancient rules taught by all philosophies might be in political law somewhere, but they are buried under mountains of made-up law, which cannot enlighten.

And, ignorance of the law is no excuse. So the typical American commits an average of three felonies per day. [2] (A felony means a year or more in prison.)

Finding right and wrong in all of that would be the ultimate "needle in a haystack."

But one of the main principles of the venerable Common Law was, if it's not logical it's not law.

Much, much different than today. Political law has no requirement for logic, or even for being ethical.

Besides, I know for a fact that you can handle Book Two because you handled Book One, and Book Two is just as easy. It's not as entertaining or heartwarming, but every bit as easy.

In fact, for normal everyday life, the basics, which are all we need, are amazingly simple. You already have their crucial foundation, these 17-Words:

Do all you have agreed to do and,
do not encroach on other persons or their property.

Highly important! Centuries of Common Law built upward from those 17-Words. They are its foundation. *Please memorize them!*

Robin, in the following dozens of letters we will clarify the details, all of which for daily life, especially your marriage, are simple and easy.

So relax. You do not need to *be* a Common Law lawyer, **you just need to be able to reason like one.** This *Owner's*

Manual will give you all you need. You will be amazed at how easy it is and perhaps how much smarter you will be. I know because I've had many lawyers and judges praise my writings about these matters. In fact, an early version of this *Owner's Manual*, written by me in the 1980s, was discovered by a justice of the Australian Supreme Court and circulated among those justices.

In my opinion, 18th and 19th century Common Law was the most important and helpful invention in all of human history. After you have been introduced to it in these letters, I suggest you go to my Uncle Eric book called *Whatever Happened to Justice?* (earlywarningreport.com/books)

Common Law was so easy to learn that in 1774 — no, that's not a misprint, 1774 — British General Thomas Gage reported that when he arrived in Massachusetts that year, he was surprised to find law was widely studied even by ordinary Americans.

Gage complained that Americans were impossible to intimidate because "they're all lawyers."[3]

Pulitzer Prize-winning historian Bernard Bailyn explains this was because Americans saw Common Law (or Natural Law) as...

"... a repository of experience in human dealings embodying the principles of justice, equity, and rights..."[4]

In other words, in those days, Robin, law was based on ethics. In fact, I might argue that Common Law itself *was* ethics.

Once you have inducted ethics into your marriage, you have inducted Common Law *reasoning*. This will be a wonderful help in running your marriage smoothly for the rest of your life.

Your Friend Rick

---

1. "Many Failed Efforts to Count Nation's...," *Wall Street Journal* website, July 23, 2011; "Overcriminalization," *Heritage Foundation* website, 2023; "Three Felonies per day", by Harvey A. Silverglate, *Encounter Books*, 2009. "Go Directly to Jail — The Criminalization of Almost Everything", by Gene Healy, *Cato Institute*, 2004, p.21 & 24.

2. Ibid., "Many Failed Efforts to Count Nation's...."

3. "Law in America", by Bernard Schwartz, *McGraw-Hill*, 1974, p.3.

4. "The ideological origins of the American revolution", by Bernard Bailyn, *Belknap Press*, 1967, p.31.

First Excerpt From The 17-Word Solution Handbook – You Are About to Work a Miracle

Letter 92

———— ✦ ————

Dear Robin,

Are you aware that a sizable percentage of the population does not know right from wrong?

Would you like to work alongside these people? Do you want them as friends?

Once you have absorbed Common Law reasoning, you will use it so often that you will soon no longer be aware you are doing it.

This is because we are talking about the simple concepts of right and wrong. I am sure many people already understand all the ideas we will cover, but in nearly every case today the ideas were learned in a hit-or-miss fashion.

They are like the pieces of a jigsaw puzzle lying in a heap on a table. We will assemble the pieces into a single clear picture. This will make them much easier to use in your marriage without mistakes.

Again, learn to think like a nineteenth-century Common Law lawyer. For everyday use, it's easy, I promise. It's a beautiful thing, and you will have it down pat by the time you finish these letters.

Of course, I am making a colossal promise. In my next letter, I will explain what qualifies me to make it.

Your Friend Rick

Who Am I to Make the Promise?

Letter 93

———— ♦ ————

Dear Robin,

Some call me the voice of experience. Born in 1946, I have led a life that has often been called colorful.

I've been a successful business owner, public school teacher, carpenter, farmer, and writer who has been published in the *Wall Street Journal*, *USA Today*, *Business Week*, and other major publications.

In the Air Force, I was a sergeant and special operations aircrew member in and above the jungles of Central and South America during the days of Che Guevara.

I have lived abroad and visited 49 states and 46 countries.

I've had more than two million words published. My Uncle Eric books, endorsed by former U.S. Treasury Secretary William Simon and other luminaries, have sold more than 750,000 copies.

Newsweek has reported that my ideas have influenced strategic planning in the Pentagon and CIA.[1]

Robin, I've been called "the 2,500 year-old-man," because some believe my experiences plus my knowledge of economic[2] history gives me the ability to view things through the eyes of a person who has lived that long.

My favorite subject is the connection between law and economics. I've made an extensive study of the economy of the Roman Empire. This reveals the connection between law and economics and has led me to coin the fundamental 17-Words.

Your Friend Rick

---

1. "McCrystal Mistakenly Reveals Secret CIA Report," by Mark Hosenball, *Newsweek* website, Oct 9, 2009 and Mar 13, 2010.

2. Economic (ee-con-om-ik): referring to the production and distribution of wealth. Wealth is goods and services. Money is the tool we use to measure and trade wealth.

Would You Like to Have Been Born in the Stone Age?

Letter 94

———— ◆ ————

D ear Robin,

That was when you would have lived in cold, leaky caves, rarely had enough to eat, had no toothbrushes or toothpaste, no modern medical care, and been lucky to survive past age 20.

Or would you prefer today's world, with its cornucopia of food, soap, swift and comfortable transportation, warm clothing and homes, beds, eyeglasses, hospitals, dentists, apple pie, and chocolate?

Do you like having an excellent chance of living past 80?

All this has been made possible by the industrial capitalism that gave rise to modern civilization. Civilization is made possible by those two simple laws:

Do all you have agreed to do and,
do not encroach on other persons or their property.

These two laws have been instilled by great teachers of law and ethics, including Socrates, Aristotle, Augustine, Confucius, and Blackstone.

Let me be clear. I am not the person who developed 4,000 years of law. I am just the guy who had the brass to boil it all down into 17-Words.

In these next letters, we will continually return to these principles. Again, they are the two that make civilization possible.

And a happy marriage.

**Do all you have agreed to do and,
do not encroach on other persons or their property.**

As far as I can tell, these 17-Words are at the heart of all professional codes of ethics, doctrines, religions, spiritual persuasions, and other philosophies.

They are perhaps the only ideas on which all agree.

They are also the only ones that are **scientifically provable**, as we shall see in a future letter.

Your Friend Rick

Legal Bedrock

Letter 95

———— ✦ ————

Dear Robin,

Over thousands of years, in all societies, the two laws became legal bedrock.

"Do all you have agreed to do" became the basis of contract[1] law.

"Do not encroach on other persons or their property" became the basis of tort[2] law and some criminal law.

The first law makes it possible for us to do business with each other — to organize our economic activity, our work, production, and trade — so that goods and services can be produced in abundance.

The first law is also absolutely, profoundly, totally essential in a marriage.

The second is our protection against savagery — against murder, theft, vandalism, rape, and assault.

In marriage, hopefully, the second law is not needed for such dire situations. But it still applies. It helps prevent arguments and hurt feelings.

The following letters will be devoted to examples and clarifications.

My goal is this, Robin: When you have finished these letters, the 17-Words will be a tool kit you can use for solving — and *preventing* — marital trouble for the rest of your days.

Samantha and I believe they are the most important element that enables a marriage to flourish.

Once the 17-Words have become part of your *automatic* thinking, you can tailor the rest of your marriage to exactly your and your lover's unique characteristics.

As you read, you might take notes to help you create a tailor-made foundational agreement, or contract, between you and the love of your life.

Even if you already have a pre-nuptial agreement, the 17-Words will make it better.

Your marriage contract can always be changed, with the consent of both parties.

In my opinion, even if you have been married fifty years and never before had a marriage agreement, you need one. That is unless your marriage is always perfect and never requires improvement.

In other words, regardless of how great your marriage is, I am confident that by inducting the 17-Words into it in specific, detailed ways, you will find it works much better and you both will be far happier and will love each other more.

Again, to have a great marriage, learn to reason like a 19th century Common Law lawyer.

"What did we agree to? Did anyone encroach?"

Your Friend Rick

---

1. Contract: an agreement.

2. Tort: under the second law, a wrong committed on someone's person or property. (Except in the case of contracts. Contracts are covered under the first law.)

Benefits of The 17-Words

Letter 96

———————— ✦ ————————

D ear Robin,

As soon as you begin living by the 17-Words — and using them to measure the behavior of others, to decide who will or won't be in your life — you will feel stress slide away.

I remember an unhappy woman who learned these two laws. She then noticed the reason she was miserable was that some of her "friends" had the habit of violating them.

She told me she began turning toward ones who were honorable, and it was as if a great burden had been lifted from her shoulders; life was fun again.

There are more benefits of the Two Laws, and I will describe them later after I have laid additional groundwork.

Everyone violates these laws occasionally, by accident. But those who do it routinely are poison. Your life will be better if you steer clear of them.

Again, *do all you have agreed to do and, do not encroach on other persons or their property.* These "Maybury's 17-Words" are the legal and ethical bedrock of civilization.

Without them, virtually everything you have goes away, including your marriage.

Your Friend Rick

Importance of Precedent

Letter 97

———— ♦ ————

D ear Robin,
   A precedent is a legal or ethical decision that is considered a guide for later decisions.

Precedent seems to be built into human nature. Every parent with more than one child runs into it: "If Johnny can go to the movies, why can't I?"

Precedent is one reason the Two Laws must always be respected by everyone. Each time someone is given the privilege of breaking agreements or encroaching, this creates a precedent for others to have the same privilege.

In short, what's good for the goose is good for the gander. Everyone is equal under the venerable Common Law and in ethics.

Especially in marriage, Robin. If one spouse goes outside the Two Laws, this automatically gives the other permission to do the same.

You might want to read that last sentence again.

One of Samantha's favorite rules when teaching children how to get along is, turnabout is fair play. If I have broken your toy truck, I've given you permission to break mine.

So, in all of your life and especially your marriage, be mighty careful about creating precedents.

Your Friend Rick

Marital Case Law

Letter 98

D ear Robin,

Precedent is also called case law. **Decisions in cases become a body of guidelines for deciding similar cases in the future.**

I imagine most marriages evolve their own collections of case law without realizing this is what they are doing. And, since they don't realize it, **they don't write their decisions down** for future reference. Big mistake. I've seen it lead to confusion and the same arguments over and over.

Here is a diagram of a system for growing a body of your case law from your disagreements.

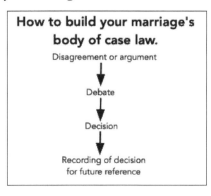

How to build your marriage's body of case law.

Disagreement or argument

↓

Debate

↓

Decision

↓

Recording of decision
for future reference

- An incident occurs and is followed by a disagreement or argument.

- The dispute triggers debate.

- The debate leads to a decision.

- The decision is recorded for future guidance.

Judging from what I have observed in my 77 years on this planet, where many marriages blunder into difficulty and heartache is in **failing to record the decisions.**

Without these references, the couple fights the same battles over and over, because they have differing memories about what was said.

Please let me disclose that the structure in the illustration is not my invention. It's how case law has operated in court cases all over the world for centuries.

The recording is crucial. I can think of few things in life that are as important. The record the partners make is their own unique body of case law *tailored* to *their* marriage!

Your Friend Rick

P.S. Notice the decisions do not contain the opinions of Uncle Fred, Grandma Connie, the neighbors, or the gang down at the local bar.

Venerable Law

Letter 99

———— ✦ ————

D ear Robin,

For many centuries, most law was about right and wrong. A case would be brought before a judge, and the judge would try to discover what was the right thing to do, based on the Two Laws, which were derived from religious principles.

A legal decision in which a new type of question had arisen, would become a precedent for later cases.

The Common Law was the body of precedents stretching back centuries. It was based on principles of right and wrong — on ethics — common to all.

In the 20th century, under pressure from socialists, the requirement for law to be based on right and wrong was erased. Today, only a tiny remnant of law is so based.

Every year, politicians and bureaucrats make up thousands of new laws, or change old ones, as they see fit. This is political law, which has no requirement to be based on right or wrong, logic, or anything else except the whims of the power holders, be they the majority of voters, bureaucrats, or politicians.

In these letters, I often draw on lessons taught by law. But I use only what I call the "venerable law" — meaning Common Law or Natural Law,[1] not politics. Not voting. Right and wrong cannot be determined by majority vote.

For over 4,000 years, venerable law — based on the 17-Words — was widely respected and obeyed, not so much out of fear, but because it was believed to be honest and just, and taught by all philosophies and religions.[2]

Robin, the 17-Words are what made the Common Law common to all.

Also, venerable law, or Common Law, is what judges were referring to when they said ignorance of the law is no excuse.

It is what Abraham Lincoln was talking about when he said,

"Let reverence for the laws, be breathed by every American mother, to the lisping babe, that prattles on her lap. Let it be preached from the pulpit, proclaimed in legislative halls, and enforced in courts of justice. And, in short, let it become the political religion of the nation; and let the old and the young, the rich and the poor, the grave and the gay, of all sexes and tongues, and colors and conditions, sacrifice unceasingly on its altars."[3]

Brilliant words. Again, Lincoln was not talking so much about political law, as about Common Law.

He was a 19th century Common Law attorney. We can be certain he would not have approved of the more than 300,000 made-up political laws now on the books in Washington, DC.[4]

I hope you will use these 17-Words as the foundation of your marriage, especially, "Do all you have agreed to do." It was the indestructible bedrock of Samantha's and my marriage agreement, and I hope you will make it yours.

Again, learn to reason like a 19th century Common Law attorney. Its basics are wonderfully easy — the 17-Words — and will be magnificent for your marriage as well as everything else in your life.

Your Friend Rick

---

1. I see Common Law as an attempt to discover and apply Natural Law.

2. "Natural Law in American Jurisprudence," Notre Dame Lawyer, January 1938, pages 89 & 90.

3. Address before the Lyceum of Springfield, Illinois, January 27, 1837. He included the Declaration of Independence and Constitution.

4. "Many Failed Efforts to Count Nation's...," Wall St. Jrnl. website, July 23, 2011; "Overcriminalization," Heritage Foundation website, 2023; Three Felonies per day, by Harvey A. Silverglate, Encounter Books, 2009. Go Directly to Jail — The Criminalization of Almost Everything, by Gene Healy, Cato Institute, 2004, p.21 & 24.

Are There Other Foundational Laws?

Letter 100

———— ♦ ————

D ear Robin,
    I coined the two laws, but some people believe in others, too.

They are certainly entitled to obey them, as long as this does not involve disobeying the 17-Words. They are ethical bedrock.

Your Friend Rick

What Makes Something Right or Wrong?

Letter 101

———— ✦ ————

D ear Robin,

The disappearance of real ethics is explored in the book *Lost in Transition* by Notre Dame sociologist Christian Smith.

What Smith and his research team learned from studying American youths, ages 18 to 23, can be summarized by the comment by one young person: "I mean, I guess what makes something right is how I feel about it. But different people feel different ways, so I couldn't speak on behalf of anyone else as to what's right and wrong."

Robin, notice the phrasing and choice of words in that sentence. This person's use of the English language shows he is not uneducated. Yet he cannot tell the difference between right and wrong.

That is what Smith and his team commonly found. Here are two more representative comments:

THE 56 YEAR HONEYMOON

- Right and wrong are "up to the individual. Who am I to say?"

- "I would do what I thought made me happy or how I felt. I have no other way of knowing what to do but how I internally feel." [1]

In his book, Smith reports that "fully one in three of the emerging adults we interviewed said they simply did not know what makes anything morally right or wrong."

In short, there are certainly lots of reasons bad behaviors are everywhere. One of them appears to be that many people have been trained to be so open-minded they have weak or nonexistent ethics.

Check your ethics and those of your spouse. Are you both clear about what constitutes right and wrong?

Have you agreed on it?

Let's start getting more deeply into this. Next letter.

Your Friend Rick

---

1. "If It Feels Right...," by David Brooks, new york times website, 12 Sep 11.

Where Did the Two Laws Come From?

Letter 102

———— ✦ ————

Dear Robin,

No one knows. There are lots of ideas, but all we can say for sure is, there they are, in every philosophy or religion, and in the venerable law of every culture, going back thousands of years.

One explanation is, they are what works. Through thousands of years of trial and error, all over the world, humans have hit on the solution that makes civilization possible: the Two Laws.

In short, the 17-Words are mine, but they represent the thinking of millions of scholars, attorneys, and judges around the globe over centuries.

I have probably studied these 17-Words more than anyone else has, and my guess is they are in our DNA. How they got there, I don't know.

But I do know they are what works for humans. Just as running works for a wolf, and flying works for a bird, the 17-Words works for humans.

The wolf can choose not to run, and the bird can choose not to fly. But they will not prosper.

The same for us, Robin. We can choose not to obey the 17-Words, but life will not go well for us.

Indeed, in Samantha's and my opinion, no marriage can be healthy without those two laws.

You may know people who are finding this out the hard way.

We are sure that if enough of us violate the laws routinely, our entire way of life will collapse.

In my next letters we will begin exploring the Two Laws in detail, starting with the first: **Do all you have agreed to do.**

The better you understand and craft your agreements with each other, the stronger will be your marriage.

Your Friend Rick

First Law – Agreements Are Contracts

Letter 103

———— ◆ ————

D ear Robin,

For most purposes, an agreement and a contract are the same thing. When, for instance, I rent an apartment or take a job, I accept certain responsibilities that I have agreed to, and the other party takes on responsibilities she or he has agreed to.

There is probably no part of Common Law as thoroughly worked out as contracts because contracts touch all parts of our lives every day. Here is a short explanation of them.

A contract consists of four parts. First is the **offer**: I will do this for you if you do that for me.

Second is **consideration**. In law, the word consideration has a different meaning than in ordinary language. It is something of value promised in return for something else of value.

• I will trade you an apple for an orange.

- I will pay you a thousand dollars per month if you will let me live in your apartment.

- If you will pay me $25 per hour, I will work for you.

- You offer to pay me a thousand dollars if I stop smoking.

All four examples are cases in which there is valid consideration on both sides: the apple, the orange, the thousand dollars, and the apartment.

On the other hand, if I say I will do such and such in return for nothing, then it is not a contract. There is no consideration on your side, so I am not legally bound by it.

Robin, contracts are about trading, not just about promises.

The third part of a contract is the **acceptance**. The person who receives the offer agrees to it freely, fully and clearly.

Fourth is a **meeting of the minds**. All parties understand and agree to all parts of the contract. They are "on the same page," or "in tune" with each other. They agree on the definitions of the words.

Contracts can be either written or oral, and they don't even need to be that. Actions can speak louder than words. What you actually do, without writing or saying anything, can create a contract.

For instance, when you go through a grocery checkout to buy a loaf of bread, your silent action of offering the money, and the clerk's silent action of handing you the bread, contain all four elements of a contract.

Do you see what I mean about contracts touching every part of our lives each day?

To me, the most important part of a contract or agreement is the meeting of the minds. Especially in a marriage. What did the lovers *intend* when they made the deal?

The *spirit* of the contract is the contract.

And marriage is, first and foremost, a contract.

Your Friend Rick

A Suggestion

Letter 104

————— ♦ —————

Dear Robin,

One discovery Samantha and I made was the more trust, the more love.

But, you must make it *possible* for your mate to trust you. To break your word even once is to damage your love affair. As I said in an earlier letter, **trust once lost is practically impossible to regain!!!**

If you are planning to make a fresh start in your marriage, I think one of the best things you can do is promise each other to let bygones be bygones. From this day forward, in all cases small and large, your word is your bond, solid gold, as dependable as the sunrise, no exceptions.

You might want to write that into your nuptial agreement.

Your Friend Rick

Tardiness

Letter 105

————— ◆ —————

Dear Robin,

   Thanks for your letter asking about tardiness.

   Here's a point crucial to your marriage as well as to your job. If I agree to meet Samantha at 4:00, and I show up at 4:15, I am training her and any observers to be skeptical about what I say. I am fostering a reputation for not being trustworthy.

   And, trust once lost is almost impossible to regain.

   I am also causing them to waste their time waiting for me, which is never looked on with favor. They may try to be gracious, saying it's no big deal, but wasting someone's time is *always* a big deal. **Time is precious, it cannot be replaced.**

   In short, tardiness is serious, don't do it.

   Now let's move on to the second law, do not encroach on other persons or their property.

Your Friend Rick

Second Law:
Do Not Encroach

Letter 106

———— ✦ ————

D ear Robin,

Everything in this law hinges upon the word encroachment.

To get a better understanding of it, let's start with — ambient levels of encroachment.

My right to swing my fist ends where your nose begins. That's a good illustration of the second law, but it does not cover all situations. Understanding ambience helps.

Ambience refers to surrounding conditions. Suppose I am in a building in a hot desert, but the room I'm in is 72 degrees. The ambient temperature of the air around the building might be 100 degrees or more, while the ambient temperature of the air that surrounds me personally is 72 degrees.

Robin, in a great many cases where the second law comes into play, there is an ambient level of encroachment. It is okay to stay within this ambient level but never go beyond it without permission.

It is okay for me to make a great deal of noise at a rock concert or beside an airport runway, but not in a church or a hospital.

I'm allowed to knock someone down in a football game, but not in a tennis match.

It's okay for me to stroll up your front walk and ring your doorbell, but not to trample your flower garden and throw a rock through your window.

If I blow smoke in a tobacco shop, that's probably okay. But if I do it in someone's private home, it's wrong unless I have the owner's permission.

A guide to what is inside or outside an ambient level is to simply put yourself in the other person's shoes. If you were them, would you be annoyed?

If the answer is yes, don't do it.

Another guide is to ask those who own the property, "Is such and such okay?"

A very good protection against accidentally going outside the ambient level of encroachment is to always be polite.

Getting married does not mean politeness can stop. Do not encroach on your mate's person or property unless you have permission. And be gentle.

Next letter, one of the most common forms of encroachment.

Your Friend Rick

Definitions & Lines

Letter 107

———— ♦ ————

D ear Robin,

In my opinion, an essential for everyone's home library is *Black's Law Dictionary*. Law, including agreements, is very much about definitions, and this easy-to-read guide first published in 1891 can be a wonderful help in everyday living.

I expect you will find its definitions a great aid in reducing arguments because so many quarrels are sparked by the imprecise use of words.

"You told me you consented. I thought you meant you were agreeing voluntarily. I see what you meant is you surrendered, you gave in. You actually felt you were being forced. I'm sorry. I would have backed away instantly if I'd known what you meant by consent."

According to *Black's*, encroachment means "to trespass or intrude."

Notice the word assumes there is a line that should not be crossed. In any case, where an assault, theft, rape, vandalism, murder, kidnapping, or any other harm has been done to a person, or to a person's property, a line has been crossed, the second law has been violated.

Incidentally, Robin, if a large number of people cross the line, this does not make it okay. Even if everyone on earth except the victim says the encroachment is okay, it isn't. The people who are doing it owe restitution to the victim.

Restitution is the act of compensating a victim for a loss or injury.

Marriage does not automatically create permission to violate either of the Two Laws. For instance, once you have said "I do," this does not mean you have an automatic right to walk into the bathroom without knocking.

My suggestion: if you want a privilege, ask for it, and specify if it is just this once or forever.

Your Friend Rick

Your Land

Letter 108

———— ◆ ————

Dear Robin,

An ancient rule is, "A man's home is his castle." You can do as you please on your own property as long as you do not let it overflow onto someone else's.

An example is pollution. If you want to ruin your own territory by dumping garbage on it, that's okay, but do not let any part of the garbage, even the sight or smell, overflow onto someone else's territory.

In short, everything we do on our own property should be contained there, and we should do nothing to anyone else's property.

So, a spouse should always take care to avoid damaging or losing the other's property.

By the way, it is my sincere belief that if the second law were obeyed, nearly all pollution problems would go away.

Your Friend Rick

Responsibilities

Letter 109

————— ✦ —————

D ear Robin,

Children, animals, and property. They do not just appear out of thin air. If I have them, I must have done something that caused me to have them.

They are, therefore, my responsibilities.

If they do harm to someone, I must restore that person as closely as possible to her or his original condition.

Even if something just appears in my life without my request or permission — a gift perhaps — if I do not remove it, I have decided to keep it, plus the responsibilities that go with it.

In my opinion, to have a child, an animal, or a thing is to accept all the responsibility that accompanies it.

In your marriage, I suggest you be clear about who is responsible for what.

Your Friend Rick

Property Is Frozen Time

Letter 110

———— ✦ ————

Dear Robin,

Suppose you are a carpenter. Someone asks you to build a table for her, and she is willing to pay you $800 for it.

The job takes you 40 hours. But before you are able to hand it over to the buyer, I break into your shop and accidentally drop a sledgehammer on it. The repair takes you another 20 hours.

"It was an accident, I didn't mean to do it. I only wanted to steal something, not commit vandalism. I got scared and fled, taking nothing with me. Since I did not intend to do damage, I don't owe you anything, right?"

Wrong.

A 19th century Common Law lawyer would ask, "Would the damage have happened if I had not broken in?"

Of course not.

So, regardless of my intentions, Robin, I'm the *cause* of the damage to you.

In marriage as elsewhere, if something happens downstream from my actions, I'm responsible. It is my duty to exercise reasonable caution. (We will talk about the word reasonable in another letter.)

I owe you $800, plus more money for your time and trouble dealing with the police and giving poor service to your unhappy customer.

My point: whether it is money you have earned or things you have produced, it is part of your life. Property is frozen time. If I have stolen or damaged it, I have stolen this time.

Never take anyone's time or property without permission, especially that of your loved one.

Your Friend Rick

More About Peer Pressure

Letter 111

—————— ◆ ——————

Dear Robin,

Here's another angle on peer pressure or majority rule. In a letter to Dr. G. Logan in 1816, Thomas Jefferson pointed out: "It is strangely absurd to suppose that a million of human beings collected together are not under the same moral laws which bind each of them separately."

And let's return to Mark Twain's remark: "Whenever you find yourself on the side of the majority, it is time to reform."

Any time I find myself tempted to cave into peer pressure, I remember those two remarks.

Reason like a 19th century Common Law lawyer. *Never* let peer pressure induce you to violate the 17-Words, especially in your marriage.

Your Friend Rick

Who Are You?

Letter 112

———————— ✦ ————————

Dear Robin,

If I am tempted to steal or violate any other part of the 17-Words, the real question at the bottom of my decision is, "What kind of person am I?"

Am I the kind who deliberately hurts the innocent?

Am I someone I would trust?

Am I someone I would be proud to call a friend?

Or hire to do an important, high-paying job?

Or loan money to buy a nice home or car?

Am I proud to be me?

Or am I the kind of person others see as poison and who isn't likely to have any friends except those who are also seen as poison?

Robin, whether we realize it or not, every time we make a decision prompted by the Two Laws, we are answering that question: "What kind of person am I?"

And because, in the eyes of the world, you and your spouse share the same reputation, you share the same answer to that question.

Next, let's look at some behaviors that are not directly under the 17-Words but are close.

Your Friend Rick

Restitution

Letter 113

———— ✦ ————

Dear Robin,

Continuing with learning how to reason like a 19th century Common Law lawyer...

If I do harm to someone, I am in debt to them. And, like it or not, the world will assume I and my spouse share the same debt.

This might not be the case legally but, again, the world generally does not see it that way. On a credit report, for instance, your name and your spouse's name can both appear, even if your spouse alone incurred the debt.

If I hurt someone, the payment of the debt is called restitution.

Robin, offering an apology is a fine thing for me to do, but it is only the beginning.

I *owe* the injured party. **I have an obligation to restore them as nearly as possible to their original condition.**

This cannot be overemphasized, especially in your marriage. These days, there are people who think an apology is enough. It's not.

In my opinion, if I harm the woman I love, the first words out of my mouth after I'm sorry should be, how can I make it up to you?

Your Friend Rick

Restitution & Fidelity

Letter 114

———— ◆ ————

D ear Robin,

By the way, Robin, I have heard lots of people say infidelity is no big deal, as long as the spouse does not find out.

If the only thing going on in the bedroom was the biological activity, this might be the case. But as mentioned in earlier letters, I am convinced that for us humans, there are emotional, psychological, and spiritual forces at work, too. Practically nothing is understood about them, so **the damage is not knowable or measurable.**

I cannot overemphasize that. No one knows everything that really goes on in the bedroom.

I remember a movie in which two male friends are at a class reunion, and one receives a tempting offer from an old flame.

His friend says, "Go ahead, why not? No one will know. We're in a different city a long way from home."

His friend answers, "I'll know."

And there is this. If I am right that there is a lot more going on in bed than just the biological stuff, is it not possible that in the case of infidelity, the betrayed spouse somehow detects it?

I think yes because I have seen it. The betrayer's personality changes.

Your Friend Rick

P.S. I can't count the number of times someone has tried to use that no-one-will-know pitch on me, especially when I was on business trips without Sam.

After I met her, I never again touched another woman in a romantic or sexual way. With one exception.

It was 1974 and we'd been married seven years, when at a New Year's Eve party at midnight I happened to be sitting next to one of our female friends. As the noisemakers went off, she turned to me, pulled me close, and proceeded to plant a spectacular kiss on me.

I confess, despite all my military training, I failed to fight her off.

Sam saw that I had been ambushed and sluffed it off.

But that was it, in 56 years it was as close to being intimate with another woman as I ever got, and I'm glad of it.

Reasonable Man Doctrine

Letter 115

———— ✦ ————

D ear Robin,

This is crucially important to marriage.

Many decisions about right and wrong depend on what has traditionally been called the reasonable man doctrine. "Reasonable man" is a legal term almost two centuries old. If you look it up in *Black's Law Dictionary* (fifth edition), you will find it under "Reasonable man doctrine or standard."

Today it is sometimes modernized into the reasonable person doctrine. I choose reasonable man because, in my day-to-day use of it, the ancient term is a reminder that this is a long-established principle, time-tested in thousands of courts as a guide to right and wrong. It was not created out of thin air by politicians. Here's how it works.

Life, including marriage, is full of gray areas in which it is impossible to make perfectly accurate judgments or measurements. In such cases, courts ask, what decision would a reasonable man make?

Robin, the reasonable man doctrine, which first appeared in England in 1837, is largely about probabilities. In a given situation, if the exact truth is not knowable, a court will ask, how should a reasonable man behave in this case?

• How would a reasonable man interpret this clause in our agreement?

• How fast would a reasonable man drive his car in this weather?

• When would a reasonable man think it is okay to defend himself?

Here is an example you can use as a reference for the rest of your life.

Suppose you and I have bows and arrows. If the patch of ground on which we stand was a giant clock, you are at 12 noon and I am in the center of the clock.

I shoot an arrow directly away from you, toward 6 o'clock.

Would a reasonable man think he is under attack and entitled to shoot back?

Certainly not. The risks to you are zero. If you shoot at me, you are outside the law. You are encroaching on me.

Suppose I shoot in the direction of 8 o'clock?

Again, Robin, the reasonable man would not feel he is in danger, and would not shoot back. If you do, you are outside the law, an outlaw.

How about 10 o'clock?

As I raise the risk, a reasonable man becomes increasingly fearful.

At 11 o'clock, a court would likely say a reasonable man would be in enough fear for his life that he would be allowed to shoot back. It is me who is outside the law, an outlaw.

Notice that in none of these examples are you a mind reader. You cannot know what my intentions are. You must observe my behavior and guess. A court would ask, did you behave as a reasonable man would?

In a marriage, the reasonable man doctrine is crucial. If one partner makes a decision that turns out badly — which is common, none of us is perfect — the other should immediately wonder, did my loved one do what a reasonable man would consider prudent?

There is a big, big difference between miscalculation and irresponsibility. Your spouse and you will occasionally miscalculate and should be forgiven. But irresponsibility can damage the marriage, or even do physical harm.

This brings us to our next subject, negligence.

Your Friend Rick

Negligence

Letter 116

---◆---

Dear Robin,

Negligence is a careless or reckless act which creates enough risk that it amounts to encroachment.

Suppose, for instance, you walk into my grocery store. You slip on a patch of cooking oil and injure your back.

Would a reasonable man expect my grocery store to be a hazardous area where he should exercise unusual caution?

Probably not. Grocery stores are generally very safe. They aren't like, say, rail yards or construction sites.

Therefore, Robin, a court could find me guilty of negligence, responsible for the damage, and order me to make restitution to you.

Without realizing it, we all do reasonable man tests every day. We don't use the term reasonable man, but he is there.

• What would a reasonable man assume are my duties in this agreement?

• I do not see any "no-parking" signs; would a reasonable man say it's okay to park here?

• Would a reasonable man say it is okay for me to walk through this person's bed of flowers?

Here's another rule of thumb: the more long-winded my argument justifying my action, the more likely a reasonable man would say it does not.

Here's a shorter one: the farther I get from simply following the 17-Words, the more trouble I am likely headed for.

And even shorter: keep my arrows pointed at 6 o'clock.

In my opinion, Robin, the habit of making reasonable man tests is more important in marriage than anywhere else. So that your spouse can be confident of your *judgment*, she or he needs to know the reasonable man test is one of your most important habits.

If a reasonable man would not do something, neither should I.

It's called maturity.

Your Friend Rick

Disputes

Letter 117

———— ◆ ————

D ear Robin,
   In case of a dispute, always go back to the Two Laws.

**Do all you have agreed to do and,
do not encroach on other persons or their property.**

Usually in marriage, it will be the first law that applies.

Ask yourself, "Did I agree to something? What was it exactly?"

What did your spouse agree to?

Did one of you drop the ball?

Did both of you?

Which of you owes the other?

Also, ask your loved one those questions. Usually, I believe, this discussion alone will settle the matter.

Marriage is a contract.

The rules of contract are one of the most important glues that hold the marriage (and civilization) together.

Robin, you need to be able to trust each other's words completely.

Putting something in writing has the great benefit of making you more meticulous and logical about what your agreements say. It's another beautiful thing.

Your Friend Rick

Do the Fundamental Laws Work?

Letter 118

———— ◆ ————

D ear Robin,

I once saw two successful businesswomen interviewed on TV. Their small firm, which they had started with very little money and not much know-how, had grown into a huge success; they were quite wealthy.

When asked about their secret, they said they always, always, always did everything they agreed to. They explained that following this rule is so unusual these days that "we got a reputation for being geniuses." It is probably an overstatement to say that always living according to the 17-Words will ensure that you will prosper. But it will give you a considerable edge over nearly everyone else since the Two Laws have practically been erased from modern culture. Unfortunately, I suspect the guiding principle today, in marriage and everything else, is don't get caught.

Your Friend Rick

Scientific Proof The 17-Words Work

Letter 119

———— ◆ ————

Dear Robin,

The most wonderful thing about the Two Laws is that **they can be scientifically proven with the accuracy of an experiment in a physics lab.**

Also, you can do the experiment yourself at any time. It's easy and fast.

Just start violating the 17-Words every chance you get. Do it for about a week, then observe the results.

What happens to your life? Does it get better, or worse?

Less painful would be a thought experiment. Take five minutes to stop and consider what it would be like to live in a world where the Two Laws are not obeyed. (I wonder if we are close to that already.)

How would you like to go into a brake repair shop where the mechanics do not believe they have an obligation to do *all* they agree to?

Or what would it be like to be rolled into a hospital surgical room where the doctors have the same opinion about right and wrong as those mechanics?

Or imagine what it would be like to live in a town where all your neighbors believe home invasion robbery and assault are a fine idea.

Robin, the Two Laws — the 17-Words — are what make civilization possible.

And marriage. I am convinced a real marriage cannot survive without them.

Again, practice reasoning like a 19th century Common Law lawyer. In everyday life it is easy. Just follow the magic formula:

Do all you have agreed to do and,
do not encroach on other persons or their property.

Your Friend Rick

P.S. Are there other laws besides the two?

I don't know. Possibly. These two are the only ones I am sure are scientifically provable.

If you believe in more, you are certainly free to obey them as long as you do not violate the two that are scientifically provable bedrock.

Again, the 17-Words are a beautiful thing, don't you think?

Using the Two Laws

Letter 120

———— ✦ ————

D ear Robin,

Whenever you find yourself in a situation where the right thing to do is unclear, return to the Two Laws — to ethical bedrock — and work your way up from there. It does not matter whether the situation is a contract dispute with a major corporation, a felony, or an argument with your spouse over where to squeeze the toothpaste tube. Robin, the Two Laws are the place to begin.

Did we agree to anything, and if so, what was it?

Has anyone encroached?

Your Friend Rick

"It is curious that physical courage should be so common in the world and moral courage so rare." — Mark Twain

Exceptions to the Two Laws

Letter 121

———— ✦ ————

D ear Robin,

If you are raising children, this might help.

There are exceptions to the two fundamental laws, the main one being youngsters.

Should babies be held to the same standards as adults? Of course not.

How about two-year-olds? Three-year-olds? Eights? Twelves?

We cannot tell exactly when the age of full responsibility arrives, because each human is different. I have seen some children whose minds developed so quickly they were responsible at age 7, and others not until 17. (And in the case of some testosterone-poisoned males, 67.)

Various thinkers and governments have tried to deal with this problem, but they have reached no consensus.

In Jewish law, the traditions of bar and bat mitzvah declare a male to be responsible at 13, and a female at 12. (I'm sure there's a message there.)

In Catholicism, the age for both is 7.

In Islam, the age is the onset of puberty, as it was in Ancient Rome.

Mormons use age 8.

In England, the age of criminal responsibility is 10, and if a child makes trouble, the parent can be fined.

In several other countries, it is as low as 7.

In U.S. law, age 18 is generally accepted as the age of legal responsibility but, again, that is just a guess. The line is drawn there simply because it must be drawn somewhere.

Robin, these letters about marriage teach right and wrong, ethics, not law — although the venerable Common Law is, in my opinion, our best source of ethical reasoning.

So, in our daily lives, we can be more flexible. I have assumed the Two Laws apply to any person whose mind has reached the age of responsibility, whatever that age might be *in each individual's case.*

You Don't Need To Know Legalese

By the way, Robin, I would argue that *every* marriage, no exceptions, evolves a body of case law made of precedents and agreements. However the partners do not understand this is what they are doing, so they do a sloppy job of it.

It's not hard. You don't need to know any legalese. Just do this.

Each time you make an agreement about something important, write it down in language the typical twelve-year-old would understand. Then sign and date it.

How do you know what is important and what isn't? One
way is to ask, "Did we argue over this issue?" If the answer
is yes, I'd judge it as important.

Please Quote The 17-Words Exactly

It took me ten years to sharpen them into a brief precise
statement. Every word of the 17 has been carefully chosen
for a reason.

Here is a definition of the word constitution, as in the
Constitution of the United States: A body of fundamental
rules or principles which a government must obey.

My hope, Robin, is that the 17-Words will act as a
simple-to-understand constitution — again, bedrock — for
a rediscovery of law based on ethics, on right and wrong,
instead of political whimsy, and on the successful operation
of marriages.

I hope the 17-Words wipe out the notion that right and
wrong are matters of opinion, or can be determined by
voting. To my mind, they are in our DNA.

**"Sometimes I wonder whether the world is
being run by smart people who are putting
us on or by imbeciles who really mean it."
— Mark Twain**

When Teaching Small Children

When teaching the Two Laws to small children, it may
be necessary to simplify. "Do what you say you will"
or "keep your word," is probably okay temporarily,
plus "leave other people and their stuff alone."

But these statements do not carry the full gravity of a binding agreement or a warning not to encroach. As the child grows, change to the more sophisticated and carefully chosen 17-Words.

Is Using Force Okay?

Robin, I have met people who believe that if they do not know how to get something important done without using force, then force is okay. This is quite insane, and perhaps the cause of much violence against spouses.

Think about it. If ignorance excuses the use of force, then the less I know, the more force I am allowed to use. At some point, if I am stupid enough, I'm entitled to do anything to anybody.

If I do not know a voluntary way to get something done, then, under the second law, my obligation is to either give it up or *keep looking* until I find a voluntary way.

Your Friend Rick

This is the end of the excerpts from The 17-Word Solution Handbook

Unconditional Love

Letter 122

─────── ♦ ───────

Dear Robin,

I am regarded as a reasonably skilled writer, but in 56 years I never found words to adequately describe my feelings for Samantha.

I realize "unconditional love" is a popular notion, and many folks long for it. But I greatly dislike the concept.

Samantha and I spent enough time helping out at battered women's shelters — an experience, by the way, I recommend to everyone, especially teenage girls — that I am convinced unconditional love is not only an unrealistic notion but a physically dangerous one.

Not, of course, a parent's love for a small child, but that is the only exception I can think of.

Robin, from day one, Samantha's and my love affair has been conditional, very much so. For 56 years, if one of us had deliberately or negligently done the other harm, the injured party would have thrown the abuser out and expected him or her to come crawling back on hands and knees.

Such an incident never happened, because we have always loved each other more than words can say. But unconditional love, no, never.

Your Friend Rick

Reasoning Like a Common Law Attorney

Letter 123

———— ◆ ————

D ear Robin,

Now do you see what I mean about learning to reason like a 19th century Common Law lawyer? Common Law was required to be logical, whereas political law, based on voting, is not.

This is not to say Common Law was logical always. Humans are not perfect. Sometimes courts made mistakes.

But that's a discussion for my book *Whatever Happened to Justice?* Among the many things it teaches, is that there was a day when the ordinary American knew, and was expected to know, a great deal about law.

Knowing about law was the same thing as knowing about ethics.

Robin, that's where the old rule, ignorance of the law is no excuse, came from.

In those days, the keystone of the law was this: **if it isn't logical, it isn't law**.

That is very different from today. Now, anything politicians and bureaucrats cook up, or voters vote for, is law.

"There is no distinctly native American criminal class except Congress." — Mark Twain

However — very important — inside your marriage, if it isn't logical, it isn't law, can still hold.

If, that is, you and your spouse agree to it.

That's the magic formula, Robin. Keep coming back to the two questions, "What did we agree to and, did someone encroach?"

These are the bedrock of civilization, including marriage. Or perhaps I should say, especially marriage.

Your Friend Rick

P.S. A close friend of mine once made the comment, "Imagine what kind of world we would have if every parent had taught every child those 17-Words."

Contracts vs. Intimacy

Letter 124

———— ✦ ————

Dear Robin,

Samantha and I found that of all the uncountable payoffs for being dedicated to the 17-Words, the most valuable to us was our 56-year honeymoon. It would not have been possible without them. Here's why.

Robin, we are completely convinced of this: **Love is mostly trust, and the 17-Words are what enable trust to flourish.**

Therefore, from what we have experienced ourselves and observed in others, the 17-Words are absolutely essential for building, or rebuilding a marriage.

That and the crucial subject of contracts prompts a revisit to the issue of bedroom spontaneity.

Life is full of obligations that require planning. But I think we should avoid planning everything because once you have agreed on a plan, it automatically becomes an obligation, a contract, a matter of keeping your word.

No one wants a life full of obligations. An obligation is pressure.

Especially, Robin, in the bedroom.

As I said earlier, I once heard a psychologist say, a great many marital problems can be traced back to one problem: he wants to and she doesn't.

A possible solution is to agree on a regularly scheduled date, say Wednesday evening or Sunday afternoon, or both. Always included in this agreement is the condition that either party can opt-out at the last minute *with no explanation.*

This might even reduce the pressure so much it will increase spontaneity. Who knows? Every person is different. Give it a try.

Also, the reduction of pressure may then add a useful sense of urgency, to seize the opportunity — to accept the offer before it expires — because the day absolutely, positively will come when the opportunity will disappear.

As it did for Samantha and me.

And you never know when that day will be.

Sam and I had only four days warning.

Thanks to Samantha's careful management of our health, and judging by our doctors' opinions as well as recent medical breakthroughs, we fully expected to live to over 110. All our long-term planning was based on that assumption.

Indeed, we believe Dr. Ray Kurzweil's statistical analyses of healthy longevity are correct. So we were actually *planning* for age 125 or even better.

But Samantha was ambushed by cancer, and only made it to 76.

Assuming Kurzweil turns out to be right in your case, do you want to live all those additional decades without the delightful entanglement of your spirits?

Your Friend Rick

A Lifelong Honeymoon

Letter 125

———— ◆ ————

D ear Robin,

This is my final letter to you about marriage.

In the days of Venerable Law, Common Law, Natural Law, or whatever you choose to call it, people generally regarded law as something to be revered.

Now law is something political, and therefore reviled, ridiculed, even hated.

As far as I know, no country's law today contains a requirement, or even a method, to discover what is truly, deeply right or wrong. So, no country's legal system can any longer be a reliable reference for identifying right and wrong, as Common Law or Natural Law once was, and is in these letters to you.

Robin, this book of letters is my attempt to help you transform your marriage into a life-long honeymoon as quickly and easily as possible.

So, again, just in case you haven't absorbed it yet, to make your marriage the closest, warmest, and most bulletproof you have ever seen, **reason like a 19th century Common Law lawyer!**

For day-to-day marital matters, it's easy. Just follow the 17-Words. In your marriage, in case of discord, ask, "What did we agree to? Has anyone encroached?"

And, always, always, always try to see things from the other person's point of view.

Your Friend Rick

P.S. Robin, I hope you can see now that the **same 17-Words that make civilization possible, make a 56-year honeymoon possible.**

After Sam got me civilized, I think I turned into a passable specimen of the male homo sapiens. Or at least I'm no longer very dangerous.

Epilogue

We Are Still One

———— ◆ ————

On a beautiful spring afternoon nine months after Samantha passed, we were sitting on the veranda talking. I said, "My love for you just keeps growing."

She surprised me by saying, "I'm glad. I need you to love me." Surprised, I asked, "But you are on the other side, how could you possibly need anything?"

It was another case of what I have run into often. As soon as Sam began conversing with me from the other side, I realized my assumptions about the other side, which I had been absorbing since childhood, haven't even been close to what it really is and what is really happening.

But her revelation about her need for me to continue loving her was on a whole different plane. She was emphatic. "We are still one. When you hurt, I hurt. When you're happy, I'm happy." She went on: "I love you as deeply as ever, and I need you to continue loving me."

And I do. We were always so thankful to have each other that everything else we had was just embellishment.

Months earlier we had come to the conclusion we are still married, and we still have work to do, spreading the 17-Words that make a healthy marriage and a healthy world possible. Her remarks on the veranda that fine spring day sealed the deal. Regardless of which side of reality one or both of us is on, the mission continues.

It reminds me of a comment by President Reagan in a 1964 speech:

"Winston Churchill said, 'The destiny of man is not measured by material computation. When great forces are on the move in the world, we learn we're spirits — not animals.' He continued: 'There's something going on in time and space, and beyond time and space, which, whether we like it or not, spells duty.'"

Samantha and I plan to continue doing all we can to spread the 17-Words, and we hope you will help in whatever ways you can.

The 17-Words — **Do all you have agreed to do and, do not encroach on other persons or their property** — they are what make possible a healthy marriage, neighborhood, country, and civilization.

Your Friend Rick

Samantha my love, I cannot possibly describe how much you are so dear to my heart.

Notes

Notes

Recommended Reading

———— ✦ ————

Black's Law Dictionary

Leonard E. Read's *I Pencil*

Frederic Bastiat's *The Law*

Bruno Leoni's *Freedom and the Law*

Oliver Wendell Holmes, Jr.'s *The Common Law*

Richard Maybury's *Whatever Happened to Justice?*

William Blackstone's commentaries on the Laws of England

Friedrich A. Hayek's *The Constitution of Liberty and Law, Legislation and Liberty*

A Simple Request From the Authors

———— ♦ ————

E ven if you do not do anything else we suggest in these letters, Samantha and I hope you will do this simple favor for us and your loved ones: three times a day – morning, afternoon, and evening, just ten seconds each — say these **17-Words,** *out loud,* to yourself.

**Do all you have agreed to do and,
do not encroach on other persons or their property!**

You will be helping make the world a better place.

Made in United States
Troutdale, OR
12/03/2024

25850715R00190